Homegrown Music

T0097744

Music in American Life

A list of books in the series
appears at the end of this book.

Homegrown Music

Discovering Bluegrass

Stephanie P. Ledgin

Foreword by Ricky Skaggs

UNIVERSITY OF ILLINOIS PRESS

Urbana and Chicago

First Illinois edition, 2006

Homegrown Music: Discovering Bluegrass by Stephanie P. Ledgin
originally published by Praeger, an imprint of Greeenwood Press.
Copyright © 2004 by Stephanie P. Ledgin. Published in paperback by arrangement with Greenwood Publishing Group, Inc.,
Westport, Conn. All rights reserved.

No part of this book may be reproduced or transmitted in any form
or by any means electronic or mechanical including photocopy-
ing, reprinting, or on any information storage or retrieval system,
without a license or permission in writing from Greenwood
Publishing Group. www.greenwood.com

Mailing addresses, phone numbers, and Web addresses were accurate
at the time this book was written, but are inevitably subject to
change.

Manufactured in the United States of America
P 5 4 3 2 1
All photographs copyright Stephanie P. Ledgin.

∞ This book is printed on acid-free paper.

Library of Congress Cataloging-in-Publication Data

Ledgin, Stephanie P.

Homegrown music : discovering bluegrass / Stephanie P. Ledgin ;
foreword by Ricky Skaggs.
p. cm. – (Music in American life)
Originally published: Westport, Ct. : Praeger, 2004.
Includes bibliographical references and index.
ISBN-13: 978-0-252-07376-2 (pbk. : alk. paper)
ISBN-10: 0-252-07376-2 (pbk. : alk. paper)
1. Bluegrass music–History and criticism. I. Title. II. Series.
ML3520.L43   2006
781.64209–dc22   2006006961

*For Dad, Norm Ledgin, journalist and author,
who has always been my inspiration.*

*And for Bill Vernon, who possessed an immeasurable knowledge
of bluegrass from which he could spin words onto paper with unmatched
elegance and who is probably reviewing an "angel band" concert led by
Bill Monroe and joined by John Hartford, Merle Watson,
Roy M. Huskey "Jr.," Ed Ferris, Raymond K. McLain, and others.
Their friendships with me will remain special treasures.*

*In loving memory of Staff Sergeant Frank T. Carvill, of Carlstadt,
New Jersey, killed in action in Iraq, June 4, 2004.
God bless you, Frank, dear friend.*

Contents

A photo essay appears following page 78.

Foreword

I first met Stephanie Ledgin nearly twenty-five years ago. But I probably had already met her, at least via the printed page, long before that without actually realizing it.

She came into bluegrass, as she puts it, by the back door, when she was hired on at *Pickin'* magazine in 1975 as one of its editors. She was not "born into the music," and she wasn't even all that familiar with it at the time. However, she fell in love with it and stayed with it all these years as a professional writer and photographer, working for numerous publications. Along the way, she became so involved in the music that she produced two successful bluegrass series in New York City and managed the career of an Italian flatpicking guitarist. Imagine that! Bluegrass in Italy! That says a lot for Stephanie's dedication—and it says a lot about bluegrass.

Bluegrass music moves people and embraces them. It comes from the heart of America yet shares its soul with fans around the world. It is symbolic of our heritage and all things American. Bluegrass is as refreshing as it is exciting. From its top-notch musicians to its excellent songs, what a great music bluegrass is to pass along to our children and to our friends.

Homegrown Music: Discovering Bluegrass is the first introductory book about America's homespun music that speaks the language of the twenty-first century. It tells you where bluegrass has been, where it is now, and where it is heading as we move along the technology highway. Well written and lively, *Homegrown Music* offers something for everyone, listeners and pickers, young and old alike. This book is an ideal "Bluegrass 101."

Get ready to explore some wonderful down-home music. When you finish reading *Homegrown Music: Discovering Bluegrass*, I am sure you will agree and understand why "Bluegrass Rules."

Ricky Skaggs
April 2004

Preface

In July 1975, I was a bluegrass newbie; that is to say, I was a relative new-comer to bluegrass music. I was a year out of college and about to accept my first full-time professional position. I had answered an ad that read, in part: "Writer/editor wanted: knowledge of bluegrass and old-time country music preferred."

I had a confident handle on my journalism skills; on the other hand, the fact that it involved the sound of fiddles, banjos, and a lively beat was about all I knew of the music mentioned in the ad. Nevertheless, with a pipe-dream desire to combine writing with some kind of music as a profession, I called to arrange an interview. I remember very well hearing music while on hold, waiting for Roger Siminoff to pick up. After some requisite prior work experience questions, Roger asked if I knew anything about bluegrass. I responded that, if it was what I had just listened to, I had heard a taste of it as a child and teenager living in southwestern Louisiana and in Kansas City, Missouri, as well as the occasional tune from any number of current folk, pop, and folk-rock groups.

By week's end I found myself engaged in a two-hour interview and tour of the offices at *Pickin', The Magazine of Bluegrass and Old Time Country Music* in Cedar Knolls, New Jersey. About ninety minutes into it, we walked past a poster with a dobro pictured, and I vaguely remember commenting on the instrument. Roger seemed pleasantly surprised to find I actually knew what a dobro was; to this day, true or not, I conjure up that moment as a defining one. I went home knowing in my heart I had the job, and, sure enough, within hours the phone rang with a job offer to become assistant editor of *Pickin'*.

Now that is not the end of this story. Remember, I was not intimately knowledgeable about bluegrass and all its finer points when I came on board the *Pickin'* staff. It had only previously touched me through peripheral happenstance.

So, what was this bluegrass newbie to do, having now to deal daily with unfamiliar and confusingly similar band names and associating the correct sidemen with the appropriate group leader? There were "Blue Grass Boys" and "Blue Sky Boys," "Clinch Mountain Boys" and a "Clinch Mountain Clan," "Lonesome Ramblers" and "Midnight Ramblers," "Nashville Grass" and "Red, White and Blue (grass)," "The Virginians" and "The Virginia Boys."

And, of course, there was the music itself. All those groups sounded alike to my virginal bluegrass ears! I had to get to know the music, its performers, the instruments, the various activities associated with it. It would be an entire year before I was "permitted" to solo representing the magazine in public at any major music function.

I stayed with *Pickin'* a little over two years, but I could not walk away from the music. In fact, I ran toward it and moved to Nashville for awhile, where a whole other world opened up to me with expanded opportunities to know more about and appreciate bluegrass. However, let me stop here with this semi-autobiographical excerpt and turn to you, today's bluegrass newbie.

The point remains, I was once a newcomer to bluegrass music; therefore, it is from that perspective that I am passing along my thoughts on exploring the very wide world of bluegrass in the twenty-first century. Perhaps you are a baby boomer whose bluegrass appetite first was whetted long ago when you heard "Dueling Banjos." Maybe you find yourself humming the theme from *The Beverly Hillbillies* after watching reruns on cable. More likely, you are one of the millions of people, young and old, who, since its release in late 2000, latched on to the music from the film *O Brother, Where Art Thou?* and started buying bluegrass and traditional music CDs in record numbers.

What is it about this American-made music that grabbed hold of me— and now you—and will not let go? I am pleased to present this forum, this book, to share with you my enthusiasm for and my knowledge of bluegrass.

Catch the excitement of where to listen to live bluegrass or find out how you can learn to pick like your favorite musician. From insight into the music's past, present, and future to its family-friendly appeal to its intercontinental attraction, *Homegrown Music: Discovering Bluegrass* will be your introductory, hands-on primer to a potential lifetime appreciation of this emotionally charged music.

Scores of in-depth bluegrass histories, biographies, and academic essays exist, some of which have been invaluable to my learning process as well as to my research for this guide. Audio-visual materials abound, from instruction to performance to documentary. In addition, the Internet has created a virtually endless outlet for exploring and sharing bluegrass. "Where to from

Here: Suggested Resources," found at the back of this book, provides numerous pathways to guide you as you enter your next semester of bluegrass.

Homegrown Music: Discovering Bluegrass is based on historical facts, prevailing notions, and on my observations of nearly thirty years as a journalist working primarily in bluegrass and folk music. I am neither a folklorist nor a performing musician (beyond my living room), and, therefore, I am able to provide a novel view of bluegrass. Because I came into the music as a newcomer, I arrived with no preconceived notions of what bluegrass is, should be, or is not, a controversy that rages even in these times, as you will read in the first chapter. The approach you will find within these pages matches my own open-mindedness to bluegrass as well as to digressive and blended forms; in that regard, the book is subjective. As you will learn, it was a sense of exploration, an expansion of musical styles, an *open-mindedness* that led to the birth of bluegrass as a genre.

Listen, learn, enjoy, participate, preserve. It is homegrown music, right in your own backyard. Discover bluegrass.

Since *Homegrown Music* was first released in the fall of 2004, several artists have passed away or retired. In addition, that time-honored revolving-door tradition of band personnel coming and going, discussed in chapter 3, has occurred and affects a few of the referenced musicians. While I have made updates to a handful of contact and Web addresses in this paperback edition, I encourage readers to use those resources listed to find new additional ones that might help you in your discovery—or rediscovery—of bluegrass. Finally, I am delighted to report that the two "rare finds" noted in "Twenty-Five Recordings to Jump-Start Your Collection" have been reissued recently on CD.

Acknowledgments

It would take another entire book to list the hundreds of musicians, fans, writers, and behind-the-scenes people I have met since 1975 who have all contributed in ways large and small to the undertaking of this manuscript. Suffice it to say, no writer is an island, to borrow from a saying.

Most would-be authors write a book and then scramble to find a publisher. I was, in fact, in the midst of doing just that, except it was not *this* book. An email came to me unexpectedly in September 2002 asking whether I would be interested in writing a book about bluegrass. For that query, my sincerest gratitude goes to Nancy Cardwell, special projects coordinator for the International Bluegrass Music Association, who passed along my name, among those of other writers, when asked by an inquiring editor. Nancy, I am flattered that you thought of me and profoundly grateful for this opportunity that you directed my way.

Thank you, Eric Levy, my editor, who, as a bluegrass newbie himself, conceived the idea for this book, approached me with that aforementioned email, then enthusiastically supported my outlined proposal for this book from day one. You had unwavering faith in my ability to get the job done during times when I had my own doubts due to life's misadventures throwing me unexpected curve balls and kittens.

To Roger Siminoff, who hired me all those years ago at *Pickin'*, thanks for the job; I certainly never imagined bluegrass would become my life's work. Our summer 2003 reunion chat meant a great deal to me and lighted my way during the course of producing this manuscript.

Hand-in-hand at *Pickin'*, Don Kissil, my editor-in-chief, kept me straight on all those Blue Grass Boys and Clinch Mountain Clan-type names. Moreover, his incredible love for the music spilled over into my heart. Thanks, Don.

Thanks to Ricky Skaggs for lending his support to this project, and to Lori Kampa, director of publicity and radio promotions at Skaggs Family Records, for facilitating. There is no arguing that bluegrass rules whenever Ricky Skaggs and Kentucky Thunder take to any stage.

My heartfelt, worldwide appreciation is extended to the multitude of bluegrass artists, other professional colleagues, friends, and family members who gave personal interviews and provided invaluable insight, information, and assistance; this book is for and about all of you.

Special thanks to Walter O'Brien, for giving me that now rare Kentucky Colonels album in 1975; to Bill Kammerzell for computer support beyond the call of duty; to Terri Horak and Martha Trachtenberg for the hand-holding chats; and to Bob Garufy and his staff at House of Equations for final prepress preparation of *Homegrown Music*.

A huge thank you for the outstanding, loving care shown by the professional and support staffs at Red Bank Veterinary Hospital and Park Veterinary Clinic during our family's cat cancer and feral cat crises that occurred during the writing of this book.

I am grateful to my parents, Barbara and Norman, for instilling in me a passion for music and writing. I feel very fortunate to have been exposed to and influenced in life by a diverse musical roster that included such names as Paul Robeson; Pete Seeger; Woody Guthrie; Harry Belafonte; Edith Piaf; Judy Garland; Scott Joplin; George M. Cohan; Peter, Paul and Mary; and the Beatles; as well as Dvořák, Tchaikovsky, and Mozart.

Finally, I could not be more appreciative and thankful for the love, support, and companionship of my husband, Ted Toskos. Your patience and understanding were extraordinary; I could not have completed this book without you. Thanks for getting up at 5:00 A.M. for an entire summer to take care of Maybelle, Guthrie, Emmylou, Mama Cass, Dolly, Patsy, Fiddle, and Banjo. Thank you for marrying me twice. Σ'αγαπώ.

Introduction:
O Bluegrass, Where Art Thou?

Bluegrass music. More a fabric of our lives than we consciously realize. For those of us who are baby boomers or older, we probably first heard instrumental music, often found in bluegrass repertoires, accompanying some of the zany goings-on in childhood cartoons—traditional fiddle tunes like "The Arkansas Traveler," "Sailor's Hornpipe," or "Ragtime Annie." And isn't that "Turkey in the Straw" the neighborhood ice cream man plays incessantly as he makes his daily rounds during the hot summer months? Moreover, who in the five-to-fifty crowd isn't in awe of Kermit the Frog's banjo playing?

Movies and television have brought bluegrass and much of its traditional roots to the forefront on any number of occasions in the last thirty to forty years. Fast and furiously driven by its banjo lead, "Foggy Mountain Breakdown" instantly brings to the mind's eye that daring duo Bonnie and Clyde as they made their bank heist getaways in the movie. From the film *Deliverance*, who wouldn't be able to name that tune, that is, "Dueling Banjos," no matter what instruments are battling?

The Dillards, a real-life bluegrass band, portrayed the hillbilly Darling Family sons on *The Andy Griffith Show*. Andy himself picked guitar and sang a traditional song or two in a handful of episodes. *Hee Haw*, which had a twenty-year run and lives on in cable rerun syndication, as well as the short-lived *Smothers Brothers*, *Glen Campbell*, and *John Denver* television variety shows all provided varying degrees of exposure for bluegrass over the decades.

In the nineties, viewers of PBS programming became familiar with "Ashokan Farewell," the recurring theme for Ken Burns's epic *The Civil War*, which featured authentic music from that era in addition to that contemporarily composed waltz tune written "in the tradition."

Internet company Yahoo! yodels its way unmistakably into our marketing minds, accompanied by equally ear-piercing banjo. Folgers Coffee and Cingular Wireless each have featured bluegrass music and musicians in commercials in recent years. In another TV ad, although we do not hear the sound from the instrument, a banjo-playing Frankenstein character touts the benefits of taking Osteo-BioFlex while playing banjo for an audience of children, demonstrating apparently that his fingers are no longer stiff.

Fast-forward to February 2002, the televised 44th Annual Grammy Awards, the honors given out within the recording industry. Surprising to artists of every ilk, let alone to those involved in the winning project, the music from the offbeat Coen Brothers' film *O Brother, Where Art Thou?* walked off with five awards, plus a sixth for a related project. The event marked the first time that nonmainstream music was recognized by the general music industry on such a scale, including capturing Album of the Year, a coveted mainstream category in which not even Nashville-produced albums had ever prevailed. This followed acknowledgment in November 2001 by Music City itself when the same top honor went to the soundtrack at the annual Country Music Association awards, Nashville thereby giving its stamp of approval to bluegrass music.

Sales of the movie's soundtrack were astonishing even by then. It charted at number six on the *Billboard* 2002 year-end chart, and a year later, by December 2003, retail sales had surpassed six-and-a-half million units.

A leading authority on the behavior of the American consumer, Simmons Market Research Bureau, in its 2003 household survey of more than 20,000 U.S. homes, found that eight million adults (over the age of eighteen) had purchased at least one bluegrass recorded product in the preceding twelve months. This was an increase of twenty-five percent over the previous year's survey figures. It was a whopping double the four million adult bluegrass consumers accounted for in its 2000 household survey.

To place a bit more perspective on its growth as well as the music industry's subsequent reaction, consider this: The venerable Grammy Awards, a function of the National Academy of Recording Arts and Sciences, did not even recognize bluegrass with its own category until 1988. Then, with the aforementioned February 2002 awards, bluegrass not only took home six trophies from one project and its offshoot, three of those nods were in nonbluegrass, noncountry slots. In fact, bluegrass and its artists took home ten awards that night in a range of areas, from roots music to mainstream, including the Producer of the Year, Nonclassical title.

Not long after, in July of that year, *Billboard* magazine acknowledged the music when it added an album chart dedicated to bluegrass; until then, only the occasional bluegrass-country crossover release had made it onto the country album chart.

Since that time, bluegrass has remained steadfastly in the public eye—and has gathered ground. And that is what is rather extraordinary. Why is bluegrass seemingly popping up everywhere and more frequently? What is it about bluegrass that has grabbed—and held—our attention as we tumble forward into the twenty-first century?

One could point to the renewed sense of patriotism that has blanketed the United States of late, a desire for Americanism and all things Americana. Such ideology perhaps refreshes our minds and rekindles memories, beckoning a return to a less complex, more heartfelt lifestyle—"a simple life," as Ricky Skaggs sings about on his Grammy-winning number.

Advances in communication and technology, particularly the explosion of Internet use, have certainly contributed to the dissemination of bluegrass, not just throughout the United States but also across oceans in such unlikely settings as Japan, Israel, Brazil, and the Czech Republic. Such innovations also present a more hands-on accessibility to the methods for learning how to play bluegrass instruments. In addition, expeditious, efficient, and cost-effective avenues for publicity have assisted in promoting bluegrass-related events, thereby ostensibly expanding its audience base.

The vehicle that propelled bluegrass into the limelight as we entered the twenty-first century, *O Brother, Where Art Thou?*, can be referenced as an inherent major factor, too. Joel and Ethan Coen, along with music producer T Bone Burnett, brilliantly wove together a tale with carefully chosen songs. The music was, in fact, central to the plot. Although not all bluegrass and not all authentic period pieces, the numbers were representative and well placed within the context. Primarily well-known bluegrass and country artists, notably Emmylou Harris and Alison Krauss, performed them.

This judicious selection and placement of roots music within the movie drew attention to the music with an exceptional immediacy. The music comprised a catalog of compositions that, when taken as a whole, had an impact like a shot heard around the world. It wasn't just the lead song ("I Am a Man of Constant Sorrow") that stirred reaction; each number held significance to its scene.

During the fall of 2000, Mercury Records' marketing folks targeted the bluegrass and country music press with advance copies of the soundtrack, getting a buzz going in those arenas ahead of its December 5 release date and that of the movie's, December 22. Bluegrass, with what could be described as its "open underground" following, and country music, with its savvy rock-and-roll sensibility, embraced it, and talked about it—big-time. In fact, more printed words about the CD appeared than comparable radio airplay, since the music was the bane of, if not banned by, major market stations.

This all being said, what sealed the deal for its success was the pure and simple fact that the music itself was—and is—outstanding. The music is captivating, not canned. It commands attention with its verve and originality. Its practitioners are believers, its aficionados fiercely loyal.

What does all this indicate? That by the time there was this increased awareness and popularity surrounding the *O Brother* music, whether we knew it or not, bluegrass already was embedded in popular culture. Only now, there were more global means (e.g., the Internet) for greater exposure. Moreover, there were media endorsements of bluegrass.

Discussion about the film's soundtrack that appeared in such time-honored establishments as the *New York Times*, as early as November 2000, affirmed that it was okay to listen to and *like* a techno-deficient, stripped down, bare-bones style of music. The cat was out of the bag. Bluegrass wasn't "just" hillbilly music. It was hip.

We discovered bluegrass has warmth, depth, and panache. Its songs are emotional, its players highly skilled. Bluegrass has a history and reflects America's roots. Bluegrass was not only rescued from the vaults and vindicated, it was validated.

Bluegrass, the music, was born in America. However, just as we are a nation of immigrants, so is bluegrass infused with influences from lands beyond our borders. We all have a family tree. Bluegrass, too, has its many origins and offshoots, or "roots and branches," a term often used in this context.

Rather than unravel and separate these twines, perhaps it can serve bluegrass better to examine their commonalities. By appreciating the similarities in the array of music that encompasses the bluegrass catalog, we can understand its significance in American music. In so doing, we can extend its reach and perpetuate the future of bluegrass while always being mindful of its past.

1

Homegrown Music: What Is Bluegrass?

Fiddles and banjos, high-speed instrumental duels, three- and four-part harmonies rendered a cappella that send shivers up your spine—American music that can quicken your pulse or melt your heart with emotion. More pervasive and present in our everyday lives than it has ever been, bluegrass is all around us. From children's cartoons to car commercials, on the small screen and the big screen, bluegrass has been a colorful thread in American music since its infancy in the 1930s.

What is this homegrown music that has captured worldwide attention, this word *bluegrass* that newscasters are no longer avoiding and that television programs and movies are working into scripts? Is it new? Is it old? Where did it come from, has it been around long, and why do we seem to be hearing so much of it lately?

Academic or textbook definitions provided by folklorists and historians tend to agree in concept. Bluegrass is considered an outgrowth of early country, grounded in string band music and derived from Southern rural—both white and black—folk traditions. Its principal identifying features lie in its vocals, all-acoustic instrumentation,[1] and instrumental virtuosity. Repertoire plays a large role in its characteristics; it also has changed the face of bluegrass, which will be discussed from a number of perspectives in later chapters.

Although often referred to as "folk" music, historically, bluegrass does not qualify, primarily because it is a modern-day form whose genesis can be pinpointed. Looking at a simplified meaning, as viewed in academia, bluegrass does not meet the criteria of folk music in that it is not "anonymously composed music usually learned through oral tradition" nor has it remained

[1]An acoustic instrument is one whose sound is not electrically enhanced or modified. In performance, however, acoustic instruments may be *amplified* via a sound reinforcement system to make them audible.

within a specific geographic community or ethnic population. Furthermore, bluegrass was pursued by its originator, Bill Monroe, as a means of earning a living, again, outside the realm of purist folk definition, where folk music is customarily performed by "nonprofessionals." And while Monroe, who is referred to as the "Father of Bluegrass," learned his craft by ear, these days players regularly, although not exclusively, learn by instruction. In academic parameters, folk artists typically have no formal training.

It can be argued that bluegrass exhibits signs of a new folk style. Legendary folklorist Alan Lomax, in a colorfully descriptive and much-referenced piece he wrote for *Esquire* in 1959, likened the bluegrass sound to "folk music in overdrive." He described and compared various features of bluegrass with jazz, and went on to give a concise historical perspective of its roots. Bringing the word *bluegrass* into mainstream view, this article was considered a turning point for recognition of the music by a wider, general, and, presumably, more sophisticated audience.

Bluegrass is, in fact, largely passed along via oral tradition—but also through modern aural means, that is recordings, audio-visual material, and, now, computer and satellite radio. Informal jam sessions engross the eyes and ears of novice pickers who bravely join in, learning on the fly. Participatory workshops are popular elements of festivals. Eager youngsters will approach bluegrass "stars" backstage and ask to be shown a lick or two.[2] Instructional materials from the "masters" are plentiful, ranging from books to DVDs, with gaps left in the audio to permit the learner to play along with the teacher.

Although hundreds of bluegrass artists get paid (on extremely varying financial scales) for making music, there are, to date, relatively few groups who actually make enough money to sustain themselves and their families without relying on a second or day job. Although a growing minority of bluegrass musicians actively pursue income from bluegrass on a full-time basis, the remainder are essentially "in it for the love of the music."

This love of the music lends itself to a sense of bluegrass community. Once you are hooked on bluegrass, you are part of the family, no matter where you land to hear it—at a mountaintop festival in Colorado, in a valley outdoor concert in California wine country, or in a cozy, unadorned basement club in New York City's Greenwich Village. So, in a broad sense, bluegrass has become folk music with its own regionally diverse traditions, handed down at pickin' parties in peoples' living rooms, local community centers, festival parking lots, and via video and computer screens in homes across the United States—and around the globe.

[2]A lick is slang for musical phrase, a complete musical idea composed of a finger and chord sequence.

THE BLUEGRASS RECIPE

In the traditionally accepted usage of the designation, bluegrass exhibits prominent lead tenor vocals, which often jump registers to reach sometimes ear-piercing falsetto. Such vocals, particularly imbued with a bluesy bent, are typically referred to as the *high lonesome sound*, a term that, over time, has become synonymous with bluegrass. Close harmony singing, in duet, trio, or quartet, is another prominent aspect. It is most evident in its bare form when observed in bluegrass gospel singing, often with spare or no backup instrumentation, that is, a cappella.

Five acoustic stringed instruments compose the core of the typical bluegrass band—mandolin, guitar, fiddle, five-string banjo, and upright bass. A sixth, the dobro, has come into popularity over the last quarter century as either replacement for fiddle or in addition to. It is important to note that, in contemporary bluegrass, electric bass can often be found. Furthermore, not every bluegrass group has the identical instrument makeup or number of individuals. Twin fiddles, for example, are often popular. There are duos (e.g., Eddie and Martha Adcock, Jim Hurst and Missy Raines) and configurations of up to six to ten musicians, such as Ricky Skaggs and Kentucky Thunder or the Lewis Family. Most often, bands include four to six members. Many musicians are multi-instrumentalists and switch instruments from song to song.

While often there is an obvious "leader" in a band (e.g., the Del McCoury Band or Alison Krauss + Union Station), every member is critical to the overall sound. This becomes quickly apparent as a song unfolds, when most, if not all, instrumentalists take a "break" between verses or chorus, playing several measures of a tune solo then giving way for the next musician to step up to the mic. The bottom line is interaction, and a successful bluegrass group demonstrates great teamwork.

Musicianship in bluegrass is not just the ability to take a break. Technical proficiency, precision, along with lightning-quick speed, such as in breakdowns (e.g., "Foggy Mountain Breakdown" also known as the theme from *Bonnie and Clyde*), are of prime importance. The degree of excellence required of bluegrass musicians is equal to that found in classical music or jazz, for example. How fast the musicians execute a tune becomes something of a competition within a band. The lead instrument on a particular number speeds up and steps ahead of the others momentarily, egging the others on to the finish line. This subtle acceleration is nearly imperceptible to the listener but almost certainly a crowd pleaser when it ends to rousing applause.

Speaking of jazz, bluegrass and jazz have a number of things in common. The genres are considered uniquely "American" music forms, created in the United States, albeit both derive from other traditions. The second commonality is that both bluegrass and jazz are improvisational. The previously mentioned instrumental breaks allow musicians the opportunity to show off their licks and let their individuality and creativity flow. Such improvisation can lay groundwork for instrumental challenges, such as those in the familiar "Dueling Banjos." Furthermore, improvisation is the mother of invention; contemporary bluegrass has taken many twists and turns, in part due to such explorations.

Suffice it to say for the moment that improvisation has expanded the definition of bluegrass over the years. Even early on, there were variations within the most traditional artist circles, in spite of Bill Monroe being recognized as the music's patriarch. Others were carrying essentially the same music to audiences but in subtly different styles. Brothers Carter and Ralph Stanley can be pointed to for their contribution of a less polished, more raw-edged presentation of bluegrass, or "mountain music," as Ralph Stanley describes it (see the following Stanley interview).

Another element that carries through to today is stage dress. Albeit not part of the "sound" of bluegrass, it is considered an aspect of the persona of traditional bluegrass. Approaching his pursuit of music as a professional means, that is, a business venture, Bill Monroe dressed the part. His was not a hillbilly or cowboy band; therefore, farm clothes and cowboy outfits from head to toe were not appropriate. After a number of years touring, Monroe and his supporting musicians settled on tasteful business suits topped off with Western hats, which has become an enduring, sophisticated image still followed by many traditional bluegrass bands. Other contemporary groups, at the very least, go with the "casual business" look, while what appears to be a minority of regularly touring bands dress to fit individualized tastes.

ADDING SPICE: BLUEGRASS CONTROVERSY

As bluegrass emerged from infancy and groups began to establish their own identities and "sounds," one particular change opened the door to questions and controversy, an issue that persists today. As might well be imagined, toting around an upright bass fiddle in a band can be cumbersome and inconvenient. In the pre-SUV era or even today, when flying to a performance, suffice it to say that transporting a double bass can present a challenge. Add to that younger musicians influenced by the relatively new electrified sounds of rock-and-roll, and bluegrass came head-to-head with the electric bass and, thus, the "what is bluegrass?" controversy began and never ended. It was further fueled when popular songs began to make their way into the repertoire, offering still another twist to this new "old" sound.

To a bluegrass newcomer, living in a world where music choices are as varied as cable channels, this might sound absurd, but to die-hard traditionalists it is serious business, likened to tampering with Mother Nature. But, then, bluegrass is not as simplistic as what is described in the preceding paragraphs. Outlined are the customary and usual features found and heard in bluegrass. The next three chapters will explore not only the origins of bluegrass but also its varied offshoots and altered states, some of which have evolved into what could be called subgenres of bluegrass; others are extensions of the music, forays into wholly other genres but performed primarily on instruments typically used in bluegrass. Repertoire, alluded to earlier, is an aspect that has grown tremendously over time. While the bluegrass catalog has not remained static, certainly scores, if not hundreds, of songs remain "standard" bluegrass fare.

What is more relevant is that controversy over whether a genre meets its proscribed criteria is not new. Jazz has many schools, from Gershwin to Django Reinhardt to Dixieland to Coltrane. The blues travel in both unplugged as well as electric circles, from the Mississippi Delta to the Piedmont region of the Eastern United States to Chicago and Memphis. Renaissance and Baroque preceded classical music, which has experienced over the centuries such movements as impressionism, expressionism, and serialism.

Rock-and-roll includes Bill Haley and the Comets, Sam Cooke, the Beatles, the Bee Gees, Sting, Aerosmith, Springsteen, Madonna, and the White Stripes. They don't all sound alike, but they all rock.

Elvis Presley, the "King of Rock-and-Roll," turned the music world upside down when he introduced a unique blend of country, gospel, blues—and bluegrass. In July 1954, he recorded and released "That's All Right," backed by Bill Monroe's "Blue Moon of Kentucky," a beautiful, slow waltz rendered by Presley in an up-tempo, frenzied style, far different from the original creation. But, rather than controversy, the songs launched Presley's career and a new spin on music.

Monroe understood that music was not just creativity, it was a business. He shrewdly embraced Presley's rendition and returned to the studio to rerecord it himself, adopting a split style to his own song, utilizing his slow waltz tempo in the first half of the number and breaking into a lively gallop to conclude. In doing so, he seized the opportunity to expand the bluegrass audience, in effect, by "modernizing" his own material.

Bluegrass is music with a message, whether contained in lyrics or in a searing banjo tune or a soulful fiddle lament. It is from the heart and always compelling. Bluegrass was built on many sounds and styles. Its influences were, and continue to be, diverse and sometimes diluted, yet there is always something distinctive about it. It is an American music that, when examined more closely, reflects this country's landscape.

Bill Monroe was an innovator who interpreted and expanded on other preexisting forms of music, honing his new work of art into an American genre. To paraphrase what legendary guitarist Doc Watson is fond of saying, if it is good music, why categorize it? Yes, there are basic elements to bluegrass, but as you continue your journey of discovery, definitive and restrictive labels will peel away.

RALPH STANLEY: DOWN-TO-EARTH, MOUNTAIN-STYLE BLUEGRASS

SPL: Since its emergence as a genre, traditional bluegrass primarily developed along the lines of three distinct styles, that of Bill Monroe, another from Flatt and Scruggs, and then the powerful, raw sounds of the Stanley Brothers. In your own words, what do you see as the difference in your style of bluegrass from those of Monroe and Flatt and Scruggs?

RS: I think mine goes back a little bit farther in what I call a mountain style or traditional bluegrass. Bill Monroe and Flatt and Scruggs were traditional bluegrass, but they were just a little bit slicker and a little bit more polished than what I do. I just do it straight from the heart, right out of the mountains. I like to call it old-time mountain music, or old-time country music, old-time bluegrass.

SPL: Why do you think the music from *O Brother, Where Art Thou?* and *Down from the Mountain* has captivated audiences everywhere and been so successful? Are you doing anything different than you were ten or twenty years ago?

RS: No, I don't think so. I'm playing and singing just like I did twenty years ago. It may have gotten a little better; I've tried my best to do a little better. But it's the same style.

SPL: Why do you think people are latching on to it now?

RS: The *O Brother* soundtrack, that T Bone Burnett produced, they spent money and put this out to millions of people that had never heard it. Where thousands heard it before—I've always done well with this music—but I've got so many new fans now, younger fans that are different. I've got my old fans and (now) a different audience. I think there are so many thousands, maybe millions, that heard it for the first time through the soundtrack of *O Brother, Where Art Thou?*

SPL: Technology, such as the Internet, has given the music a huge boost, that and the money and effort put into its marketing.

RS: Right, that's what I think.

SPL: This book is aimed at newcomers to bluegrass music. What would you want to say to them to encourage them to listen to more bluegrass, and what would you suggest for them to listen to?

RS: There's several different styles of what they call bluegrass now. I like the traditional, which I play, the traditional. There's very few today that play traditional. There's some they call progressive. I'd tell them to listen to the progressive and the traditional, and pick which one they like.

SPL: If you could play only one song for a group of people who had never before heard bluegrass, what song would you choose and why?

RS: That's a hard question right there! But I like "Pretty Polly." There's several I could name, but you said one. That's the old-time mountain sound right there; that's what I like.

SPL: One that I came to love when I first started listening to bluegrass was "Clinch Mountain Backstep."

RS: Well, now that would be good, that would be good! *(Laughing)* Let's listen to both of them!

SPL: Why is bluegrass music so important in the realm of American music?

RS: It's more down-to-earth. It tells a story; a lot of the songs do. It just fits all classes of people. A lot of the music doesn't suit old people or real country people. Well, this type of music has not only reached the old people and the mountain people, it's gone out now and proved itself to the world. I think it's a good reason for it.

SPL: As a performer of traditional music, how do you keep traditional music fresh?

RS: You know, I've been at it fifty-six years, and people tell me this is just as fresh as it ever was. And I've done the same style. A different song, maybe say, country music, they hit big and sell a million copies. Well, next year, most of the time, they're gone. Songs that I recorded fifty years ago, people still like 'em. I don't know why it is. They don't sell a million overnight. But they sell for fifty, sixty, seventy years. And they'll probably be a-selling a long time after I'm gone. It's just a sound they can't get out of their mind.

Interview conducted January 21, 2003, McCarter Theatre, Princeton, New Jersey.

2

The Evolution of Bluegrass: A Mosaic of Influences

"We can't know where we're going until we know where we've been." These are the words of Emmylou Harris, a star whose music has covered traditional roots to electrified country rock.[1]

The history of bluegrass music is filled with a rich, colorful tapestry of tradition. Much of what is defined as bluegrass, or recognized under the bluegrass umbrella today, is largely dependent on its roots, the musics from which it grew and from which it is borrowed. And sometimes it is difficult to untangle these roots from the main "trunk" of bluegrass.

As explained in chapter 1, in the purist's book, bluegrass is not considered folk music. Yet, it did evolve from a number of true folk traditions, those of early Anglo-Americans as well as of African slaves, later free blacks. However, even these traditions are racially mixed to the point where there is not always a clear-cut division of whose music was the "original."

This could also explain why a lot of the music lays claim to multiple sources, leading to varying versions and titles. The same song or tune often had a "white" interpretation in addition to a corresponding "black" rendering. Today, we have modern technology to help spread music across communities and cultures. More than a century ago, the lack of such audio or electronic technology likely encouraged people to, at the very least, get out and listen to, as well as share in, music. In mountain areas, whites and blacks were neighbors; music and dance were often "community" events.

Among the material brought over by early settlers were age-old English ballads and timeworn fiddle tunes of the Celtic Isles. Many immigrants were highly artistic, coming from the culturally developed areas of northwest

[1]Quote observed painted on a wall at the end of the "Sing Me Back Home" exhibit, Country Music Hall of Fame and Museum, Nashville, Tennessee, February 2003.

Europe. Their ballads spoke of love and family. They conveyed true-life stories, hard times, death, and other miseries.

Fiddle and guitar were known to be found regularly in the Colonies. Guitar, though not exclusively, was a popular ladies' instrument, with "parlor" guitars in vogue to accommodate women's smaller hands. Not only was music for listening, it was also for dancing. Dance was an integral part of social life, carrying over from the British Isles and beyond. Formal English dances transformed into looser country set dancing once they hit the shores of America.

Perhaps you danced "The Virginia Reel" in elementary school? This reel is a form of contra dancing derived from Scottish longway dances, which involve several couples lined up facing each other. A running set, or Appalachian square, developed from this in the mountain regions up and down the East Coast, while later square dances evolved primarily on the West Coast and in Canada. In some cases, stylized moves and a variety of footwork were added, leading to other more contemporary styles. The tunes played for these dances were typically lively fiddle numbers whose names varied the farther they got from Ireland and Scotland. Dance played a pivotal role in the development of bluegrass, as you will discover in chapter 3.

George Washington was said to have had a favorite fiddle tune, "Jaybird Sittin' on a Hickory Limb," while Thomas Jefferson's was reportedly "Grey Eagle." Jefferson himself was an avid musician and practiced fiddle daily, drawing from both classical and popular repertoires. A 1947 article, by Louis Biancolli in *Life* magazine, described how, during the course of his travels, Jefferson had his fiddle with him when he spent a night at Patrick Henry's house. Upon request of his host, he played. Henry reportedly was so moved that he got up and danced a jig. Jefferson courted his future bride, Martha Skelton, with fiddle playing.

African slaves brought over and developed their own folk traditions and music, including the *banjar* (also *banjer, bangie, banza*), the forerunner of the banjo. Thomas Jefferson took special notice of a *banjar*, giving a detailed description of its construction in a 1781 journal. Slaves were often known to build their own instruments. Fiddle was also popular among them.

Even on slave-owning plantations, there was interaction between blacks and whites in music and dance. Blacks would be called on to provide musical entertainment or accompaniment for colonists' social dances and functions held in their homes and towns. In the late 1800s and into the twentieth century, rural black musicians, sometimes known as "songsters," would travel a regional circuit and play for community country dances, white and black. Fiddle and banjo both seeped into the development of black spiritual music. Later, the dual sounds of fiddle and banjo would become entrenched in the white traditional playing known as "old-time" music, a rough-edged, raw sound reflective of the simple country life.

By the middle of the nineteenth century, the banjo had been modernized, frets and a fifth string added, which provided the opportunity for syncopation. It gained increased public attention and popularity, mostly through the proliferation of minstrel shows. Whites in blackface denigratively mimicked blacks' mannerisms and speech, as well as their music and dance. While now, in retrospect, we see how socially rude and damaging these exaggerated portrayals were, the fact remains that this was one more vehicle by which music and dance continued to "cross over" and integrate.

It is important to understand how the banjo was and is played to place it, as I will do later, in the bluegrass perspective. History indicates that early African Americans used the banjo mostly as a rhythm instrument. What is referred to synonymously as "clawhammer," "frailing," or "mountain-style" banjo is so designated as a result of how the banjo is played. In this "old-time" technique, the banjo is "brushed," or strummed, with a fierce down-stroke, using the back of the nail of the index or middle finger(s) while loudly plucking the fifth (top) string with the thumb immediately on completion of the above brushing. The wrist, as opposed to the fingers, initiates all the action, while the hand and fingers remain in a cupped, clawlike position. The results are highly percussive. It is a very different sound from the readily distinguished individual notes sounded in "bluegrass" banjo playing.

Toward the end of the nineteenth century, banjo players began to adopt a two-finger picking action, imitating the plucking of a guitar. Minstrels employed both methods, helping to further the new finger style. Although it is unclear precisely when, where, and by whom it was initiated, around this same time another technique began to appear. This approach used three, as opposed to two, fingers to pick banjo, crisply sounding out individual notes in a fast "roll," an *arpeggio*, that is, playing out a full chord rapidly note for note (as opposed to strumming the chord). It is known that this three-finger method was prevalent throughout western North Carolina and bordering states. Furthermore, by this time, the banjo was more closely associated with white musicians. Blacks had begun to favor guitar, which had become more widely available through mail order.

At roughly the same time, as well as a little earlier, music of the black communities had begun to emerge that reflected their social circumstance, not unlike that of poor or rural white neighbors. Their own true-life ballads were created, many of which survive today in folk, blues, and bluegrass genres. Chants and work songs grew out of the need to overcome the tedium and monotony of hard, long days spent at physical labor. Workers would use a song to support and encourage each other while performing repetitive tasks, such as hammer blows while laying train tracks. The song's tempo would set the pace for performing their arduous work. The work song known as "call and response" was one such development, a structured piece that would have a lead off by one individual followed by unison singing "in response."

During the Civil War era, blacks devised songs to communicate in code Underground Railroad escape routes and plans. Other songs graphically depicted work life and some of those laborers.

"John Henry" is one well-known ballad adopted by many over the years. Originally written by black workers on a rail line, it is based on a true tale and is a good example of the oral folk process. Over time, its renditions have been altered to meet specific genres. Passing from the black community where it was composed, it was introduced into the old-time repertoire, was popularized as a sixties folk revival song, and is now commonly performed by bluegrass artists.

Before the beginning of the nineteenth century, black sacred music was largely ensconced in that of whites, most blacks having been indoctrinated in white churches. Hymns had become standard fare for whites and blacks alike in the middle of the 1700s. But by the early 1800s, camp meetings began to change the face of worship music. Two to three thousand attendees would come together to worship under large tents erected for the weeklong camp meetings. Here, whites and blacks shared prayer and sacred songs. Highly emotional, spiritual songs materialized, primarily among black congregants. Taking the original European melodies, black worshipers would adapt them to lively, "uplifting" fiddle tune rhythms. These spiritual songs continued to cross color lines, finding their way into both black and white sacred repertoires. Widely acknowledged as being of black origin, spirituals were the genesis of gospel music.

In 1871, the now world-famous Fisk Jubilee Singers of Nashville began to tour to raise funds for all-black Fisk University. Performing primarily for white audiences, they shared spirituals throughout the United States and in Europe, introducing legions to the beauty and depth of what would evolve into modern gospel in the twentieth century.

Much of bluegrass gospel today draws heavily from a repertoire that is difficult to distinguish from its white versus black origins. Stylistically, however, the Nashville Bluegrass Band, formed in the early 1980s, probably follows the black gospel school more closely than other contemporary bluegrass groups. The band members accomplish this not just in the material they perform but also in their rhythms and interpretations. By accurately capturing and emphasizing each syllable of every word sung, they reproduce faithfully the spirit of a cappella gospel. Their inflection and harmonizing capture the genre so well, one would be hard pressed to know who is singing—white or black—when listening to the band's recordings, for example, with the Fairfield Four, the legendary black gospel ensemble. One can discern these very similar affectations in fifties "doo-wop" music.

Adversity and challenges of the time were the impetus behind early blues, which sprang from black communities around the beginning of the twentieth century. It was as soulfully expressive as their spirituals, yet somewhat "countrified." In rural areas, whites and blacks were neighbors, which opened the door to sharing in each other's music.

The blues reflected any number of styles and influences; however, it is steeped in its own type of folk balladry. Stanzas, for example, were less formal than the linear ballads that sprang from the Anglo oral tradition. Blues lyrics were less structured, less poemlike. One could well imagine the singer sitting on a back porch casually telling a story, which could very well be how many were derived. As blues developed, the music differentiated and became more distinctively "black," less "rural white." It took on regional characteristics reflective of blacks residing in the Virginia and North Carolina Piedmont areas, the Mississippi delta, and other geographically defined quadrants.

As much as music is a part of our modern leisure lives, it was even more important socially and culturally a hundred years ago. In many instances, it was an essential component to family and community life. Immigrants brought with them customs and traditions steeped in family, religion, and ethnic idiosyncrasies unfamiliar in America.

To keep alive one's heritage, "old world" music, food, and handiworks remained central to family and community gatherings, especially in rural areas. Far from urban entertainment and diversions, people had to create their own. They did so with music and dance brought over by their ancestors, now blended with American ones. New neighbors and friendships created opportunities to share cultural traditions, including exotic-sounding foods and music that readily made their way into the fabric of rural American life.

During this period, Anglo folk traditions continued and flourished. Hints of other European traditions increasingly showed themselves. Invented in Germany but popularized in the United States, the autoharp, or "chorded harp," was introduced in the late 1800s. It was relatively easy to play, and women especially found it accessible for its grace, style, and size. It took its place alongside guitar as a folk instrument. In mountain and other rural areas, the lap-style dulcimer—also known as the mountain or Appalachian dulcimer—was often employed for rhythm accompaniment. Ethnic versions of this "sweet songs" instrument—as the name translates from the Latin—were found in Scandinavian, German, and Dutch families. Fiddle and banjo continued to hold their rightful places.

A NEW CENTURY BRINGS NEW MUSIC

Two-hundred-year-old ballads and melodies survived as the twentieth century was born. These folk songs, handed down from generation to generation, would surface renewed at times with updated lyrics or an altered melody, or with new words to an old tune. Many took on fresh relevance as occupations, such as coal mining and factory work—and conditions associated with them—mirrored those of earlier times across the pond.

At the turn of the twentieth century, a number of factors occurred that would lay the final groundwork for the development of bluegrass, still some years off. Jazz, America's first homegrown music, was born. It was an improvisational style derived from black folk and blues, colorful Latin American sounds, ragtime syncopations, as well as numerous other contemporary music popular around 1900. Jazz could swing as beautifully as it could be sultry or blue.

In addition, the advent of commercial recordings provided the opportunity to listen to music in one's own living room. Close on its heels, radio expanded the reach of music exponentially, bringing many types of music to a coast-to-coast audience.

Among the earliest recordings were those of old-time fiddlers and string bands sought out by entrepreneurial record producers, among them Ralph Peer, who would later become responsible for some of the most successful artists of that era. "Race" records brought African American blues artists as well as ethnic performers to greater public attention.

Recordings were generally performed in an unembellished, unsophisticated style. However, there were some that exhibited more polish and tight ensemble playing.

The Shelor Family of Virginia, also known as Dad Blackard's Moonshiners, recorded fewer than half a dozen sides in the 1920s. They returned to their everyday lives, never to record again, yet they are an early example of an enduring quality still largely found in today's bluegrass groups, the family tradition. Even if music had not been pursued outside a family for two, three, or four generations past, a large percentage of today's bluegrass musicians cite having been influenced by or directly learning from one or more family members who played and passed on the music. Sammy Shelor, banjo player since 1990 for the Lonesome River Band, is one such musician. In his early forties, Shelor provided some colorful insight into his family's music and its influence on him when I interviewed him in October 2003. Related more closely to the Blackards, he explained that Dad Blackard's sister married his great-great-grandfather Shelor:

> Dad Blackard's Moonshiners consisted of Joe Blackard, Clarice Shelor and [her husband] Jesse Shelor, and his brother, Pyrus Shelor. Clarice was Joe Blackard's daughter. According to Jesse's son, James Shelor, Dad Blackard made up the "Moonshiners" name on the spot while in Bristol, because they had to have some name for the recording.
>
> Clarice played piano and she would play fiddle tunes [on the piano]. I would go to their house when I was just a small child and pick with them. This was the late sixties, early seventies. [Clarice] was a really large lady. When she would play the piano, she would move, and the floor would move in the house! But she could play fiddle tunes note for note. [She would] play the bass lines and the rhythm chords with her left hand and play all the melody with her right hand. She was one of the most amazing piano players I've ever seen in my life.

I mean, this was deeply rooted in old-time music. They lived in Meadows of Dan, Virginia. I grew up in that area and they were a big influence on my early music.

My grandfather was Cruise Howell. He played banjo. My great-grandfather, Jeff Howell, was an old-time fiddle player and had a mill and also made moonshine. When Charlie Poole would come through, he was looking for a drinking partner.[2] So he'd always go to my great-grandfather. They would drink and play. And my grandpa learned to play banjo from Charlie Poole. [But] he quit for years and then when I was born, he got interested in it again and got me started in it. So I started playing when I was five. And my other grandfather, Sandy Shelor, who's ninety-six now and lives with me, he used to take me different places to play and got me exposed to a lot of different music.

Around the turn of the twentieth century, mandolin was brought to the United States, primarily by Italian and Eastern European immigrants. Inexpensive ones began to be constructed and were sold through mail-order catalogues. Mandolin playing took hold quickly and became something of a phenomenon, heard regularly in vaudeville and on college campuses. Mandolin orchestras sprang up, which, in recent years, have seen a revival in this country.

When broadcasting took hold, radio stations sought out performers to appear live on air. Some of these were the same artists who made recordings. The radio and recording industries thus began their long-term codependent relationship. Along with this came not only wider distribution of both white and black genre music but also the opportunity for these music forms to be heard in each other's camps. Mutual musical influence was just a few notes away.

There were many talented artists who were active during the 1920s recording era, some who went on to prominence in a variety of arenas, including the *Grand Ole Opry*. However, two stood out for their tremendous successes. Their careers helped set into motion the commercialization of "hillbilly" and early country music, contributing in different ways to the development of bluegrass.

Jimmie Rodgers was famous for his yodels and train songs, hence the monikers the "Singing Brakeman" or "Blue Yodeler." As the first major country artist to have a hit recording, Rodgers brought the genre into the popular realm. "T for Texas" (or the "Blue Yodel") captivated the nation and launched commercial country music. His expressive, warbley vocalizations would find their way into the makeup of the bluegrass

[2]Banjo-playing leader of Charlie Poole and the North Carolina Ramblers, recording artists who gained considerable popularity in the late 1920s and who employed a three-finger banjo picking style that was beginning to emerge from that region and that would later be adapted to and adopted as key to the bluegrass sound.

sound. It was Rodgers's interpretation of "Mule Skinner Blues," a telling and insightful song about the work of mule-driving teamsters, that would become the signature piece for Bill Monroe a few years later.

Jimmie Rodgers had taken part in the legendary Bristol (Tennessee) sessions of 1927. Also part of these historic recordings was the Carter Family. Husband and wife, A.P. and Sara Carter, along with Sara's cousin, Maybelle Carter, who was married to A.P.'s brother, carried music from their southwest Virginia homeplace to a newly developing national audience. They shared the music they had grown up with in their families and community, messages and themes that touched hearts and souls everywhere.

The music of the Carter Family is timelessly embedded in the patchwork of American music. With nearly three hundred songs attributed to their catalog, theirs remains one of the most significant, far-reaching repertoires. Their songs surface in recordings of nearly every genre. Bob Dylan to the Grateful Dead have acknowledged their influence.

A.P. would go away for days "collecting" songs from friends and strangers alike, anyone willing to share with him tunes handed down for generations in a family. It is unclear to this day how many songs copyrighted by A.P. Carter were ones he adopted or adapted from hymnals of the day, from traditional ballads, and from popular songs dating to the late nineteenth century. Many of these have become standards in the bluegrass repertoire, for example, "The Storms Are on the Ocean," "Gold Watch and Chain," and "Will the Circle Be Unbroken."

Influenced in part by her banjo-playing mother, Maybelle Carter left her mark with a distinctive guitar-playing style. It is one of the most frequently copied by bluegrass and other acoustic guitarists, and, at the very least, heavily leaned on by others. Having also observed the guitar playing of Lesley Riddle, a black blues guitarist and A.P.'s friend, she developed a novel approach in which she would manage to cover both the lead notes as well as the accompaniment in one fell swoop. Sometimes referred to as "drop thumb," "thumb brush," or simply "Carter style," it was first popularized— now immortalized—on the Carter Family recording of "Wildwood Flower."

The children of both original Carter Family couples were involved at various times and in different capacities in the making and presentation of the Carter Family music. Perhaps best known was June Carter Cash, wife of country star Johnny Cash. June was Maybelle's daughter. Sara and A.P.'s daughter, Janette, in seeking to preserve her family's music, built and continues to run, along with brother Joe, a six-hundred-seat theater. Nestled against the backdrop of the Clinch Mountains in Hiltons, Virginia, is the Carter Family Fold, where, since the mid-1970s, they have kept "old-time acoustic mountain music" alive. Artists of local and world renown take to the stage weekly to share and continue the circle of tradition unbroken. In the following interview, Janette Carter shares a personal reminiscence of her family's legacy.

JANETTE CARTER: TAKING CARE OF THE ROOTS

In October 2002, Janette Carter traveled to Louisville, Kentucky, direct from England, where she had participated in a conference studying and honoring the music of the Carter Family. Heading toward eighty years of age, she flew all night to be able to attend the annual World of Bluegrass awards luncheon where she was to accept the Distinguished Achievement Award, presented by the International Bluegrass Music Association (IBMA), "in recognition of pioneering accomplishments that have fostered bluegrass music's image and broadened its recognition and accessibility."

Her travel fatigue was somewhat erased by her visibly heartfelt joy in receiving this honor. I was thrilled that she spontaneously agreed to share a few precious minutes speaking with me. I had met her previously only once, in August 1982, at the McLain Family Festival near Berea, Kentucky. Her pride in her family's musical accomplishments was evident as she spoke in her relaxed, down-home manner. Often continuing beyond the question, she reminisced about her family, recovering from her memory bits and pieces that she chose to share.

SPL: Why do you think the music of the Carter Family originally grabbed the attention of the entire country seventy-five years ago?

JC: It was so pure and they worked so hard at it and they believed in it, those songs and things. Each one was a good piece of poetry put to music. You could hear the music and the chords; it wasn't just thump, thump, thump. It told a story, usually a ballad or a love story or hymn or a blues. Whatever it was, you could tell it was the Carter Family.

It always amazed me how they could get that much music—that would last seventy-five years since they started—just two little instruments to get all of that music out of. I heard Aunt Maybelle say that Daddy told her, he said, "Now, you're going to play the guitar. I want you to pick it *out*, so that people will know what you're playing even if you don't sing." So she did what he told her to do. There's never been anybody that was copied any more than Maybelle's guitar playing. And my mother's singing voice, nobody ever could equal. And Daddy had such a beautiful voice. I wish he had a-sung a lot more solos and done a lot more than he did. But he had a beautiful bass voice. I mean, he could sing high; he could sing low. They had beautiful harmony, too.

And they worked and they worked, and it was very hard what they did. But I've heard 'em say that when they made records, they never had to do the record but one time. They went through it and when they got through, it was a record. They didn't…make mistakes. They were professionals. [But] they didn't know, they had no idea the impact that they were putting on music. They didn't know what they were a-doing. Neither did [Ralph] Peer who took all their songs and helped them all through the years, seventy-five years, that's a long time.

SPL: Where would you like to see the music of the Carter Family and bluegrass music twenty-five to fifty years from now?

JC: I hope it'll still be a-going, going strong. It may have some slowing down. But it'll come back to the front, because it's the roots. I'm a-trying my best to keep the roots alive of old-time music [at the Carter Fold]. If you take a tree, if you don't keep its roots wet, it'll die. And if you have that, have those roots, it will branch out, some may be big branches, then slow down, branch out some more. But it doesn't die as long as you take care of the roots. That's the way I look at it.

Interview conducted October 17, 2002, World of Bluegrass Trade Show, Galt House, Louisville, Kentucky.

3

Banjo Meets the High Lonesome Sound

Just as it was enmeshed in the cultural and social lives of so many others in the region, so, too, was music in the family life of Kentuckian Bill Monroe, born in 1911. It is important to glimpse into the life of the "Father of Bluegrass" to understand further the music's developmental path.

Cross-eyed and teased as a child, he enjoyed the gift of music courtesy of his mother, who sang and played button accordion, harmonica, and fiddle, and her brother, Uncle Pendleton Vandiver, who was a fiddler for local dances. Monroe's father could dance well, and this talent was inherited by the father-to-be of bluegrass.

Music made in the family was supplemented by what was heard and sung in church. It was a large family, and the four youngest Monroe children demonstrated the keenest interest in playing music. Bill's sister Bertha took up guitar, as did brother Charlie, while another brother, Birch, played fiddle. Bill was the youngest and by "default" ended up with mandolin, although he first pursued guitar and fiddle.

Completely orphaned by his mid-teens and his siblings largely gone out on their own, Bill lived for several years with his Uncle Pen, from whom he learned much about life and music. Uncle Pen's fiddling became a heavy influence on the music Bill would cultivate into bluegrass. Years later, he was known to pull from his memory the notes and phrasing of Uncle Pen and convey them to fiddlers who passed through the ranks of Blue Grass Boys, wanting them to capture the same spirit and sound in their playing. These dance rhythms became the backbone of the drive found in Monroe's bluegrass music.

From about the age of twelve, Bill had accompanied his Uncle Pen on guitar at dances. It was during this same period that he met a local black blues guitarist-fiddler, Arnold Shultz. Monroe would later acknowledge other realms of black music, including gospel, as influences. The great impact of

Shultz's style, which leaned toward jazz, is evident in the soulful vocalizations and syncopated delivery of Monroe's bluegrass. Other white players from the region trace their technique to Shultz as well. Inscribed on his gravestone, Shultz's guitar picking is described as "dedicated to thumb picking and finger cording [*sic*]."[1]

By the early 1930s, Bill and brothers Birch and Charlie had each moved north to the greater Chicago area for oil refinery work. There they also found spots as square dancers and as musicians for community events in the local theaters, sometimes taking on work in Midwest regional road tours. In reality, dancing all but paved the way, opening doors to other opportunities to perform music as time went along. Through virtually his final days of performing, when already into his eighties, Bill Monroe would almost always break into at least a few buck dance steps on stage midsong. He was known to call up to the stage or grab the nearest woman in sight as a spontaneous dance partner, twirling and sweeping her off the floor, never missing a beat. Monroe was a tall, imposing figure yet an incredibly graceful dancer.

As explained in the previous chapter, dance was as much a part of hillbilly and early country music as was the playing of it. It was woven into the social fabric. Square dances were popular, and fancy footwork was the hallmark of a good square dancer. These steps incorporated buck dancing while going through squares' routines.

Buck dancing, or flat footing, derives from a combination of influences. Slaves brought with them from Africa distinctive dance moves, which evolved into what were known as "shuffle dances." The buck-and-wing is one such shuffle dance and was first popularized in nineteenth-century minstrel shows. At the same time, Irish step dances and jigs, along with English clog dances, such as those danced wearing wooden-soled shoes to northern Lancashire and Liverpool hornpipes, met head on with the buck-and-wing. Rural folks grabbed a bit of each. In mountain communities, barefoot flat footing took hold and resembled more of the shuffling, close to the floor, style. Buck dancing is essentially the same but exhibits more movement of the arms, legs, and knees, a "loose limb" effect, and it is generally danced in shoes to accentuate the beats against the floor. Modern tap dance derives directly from all the above.

During this time, Bill's exceptionally fast mandolin playing was receiving much notice by fellow performers on the circuit, but the role of the mandolin still took a backseat to the fiddle and vocals. Bill Monroe was not satisfied, wanting to capture with mandolin the spirit and notes of his Uncle Pen's fiddle playing.

By 1934, circumstances were such that Bill and Charlie set out to work full-time as a duo, the Monroe Brothers, while Birch stayed behind to work

[1]For a photo of the Shultz gravestone, see http://www.aawc.com/images/family/photo19.jpg.

and help support others in the family. Touring brought opportunities to hear variations in hillbilly and country styles played by musicians from neighboring states. Of particular note, North Carolina bands were carrying banjo players who used a different technique to pick, a three-finger style rather than the older two-finger attack.

It also brought the Monroe Brothers enough notice and popularity that, in early 1936, it landed them their first recording session. On the Bluebird label, the first song among others they recorded, "What Would You Give in Exchange for Your Soul?" would become their biggest hit. Guitar and mandolin "brother" duos were popular, but the Monroes began to pull ahead of the pack and attract more attention with their snappier, faster delivery of songs. Bill's mandolin playing had begun to take on a new, lead instrument dimension.

A BROTHER ACT DISSOLVES, THE BLUE GRASS BOYS EVOLVE

By early 1938, Bill and Charlie parted, sibling rivalry getting in the way of their career as a team. Charlie went on to form his Kentucky Partners. After several months and a couple of false starts, Bill ultimately emerged in 1939 with his own group, Bill Monroe and his Blue Grass Boys, taking a cue from the nickname of his home state.

However, the music was not yet sculpted into what would become bluegrass nor was it known as bluegrass. Nevertheless, it was a good act, so good that Bill and his new band auditioned for the *Grand Ole Opry* in Nashville in October 1939 and won the spot for life. One of the songs he chose to audition with was Jimmie Rodgers's "Mule Skinner Blues," which was also the first song he ever played on stage at the *Opry*. Monroe upped the tempo and added his own spin. It would remain his signature song for the rest of his days.

For the next few years, Monroe continued to hone his sound, working up four-part harmony gospel numbers as well as perfecting the art of improvised instrumental breaks. Part of the Monroe style also thrived in the entertainment value of the act; early on, Bill's showmanship gave him an edge over others. In 1942, Bill Monroe and his Blue Grass Boys expanded to a five-person lineup, adding banjo alongside mandolin, fiddle, guitar, and upright bass. Several personnel changes would take place before the bluegrass sound would gel.

The 1940s witnessed war years, and some of Monroe's musicians came and went as a result of military service. The final pieces of the bluegrass puzzle would fall into place during 1945 and 1946. The configuration of the Blue Grass Boys that melded during this time frame provided the backdrop to the music that would later be called bluegrass. Chubby Wise was an extraordinary fiddler who took his Western swing-inflected playing and applied it to Monroe's bluesy mandolin licks. Howard Watts, who performed under the name Cedric Rainwater, was a comedian and bass player whose jazzlike "walking bass" technique would be utilized by many bluegrass bass players over the years. Tennessean Lester Flatt played guitar in a fluid but emphatic style, reminiscent of that of Maybelle Carter's. He wrote songs and sang lead, complementing well Monroe's voice on harmonies. And from North Carolina came a young five-string banjo picker by the name of Earl Scruggs.

They say if you shake a tree in North Carolina, a banjo picker will fall out. Many of those pickers in the mid-1930s and into the 1940s were employing a three-finger roll rather than a two-finger method to play banjo. While most cite Snuffy Jenkins as popularizing this technique, largely through widespread exposure from regional radio appearances, virtually all agree that it was Earl Scruggs who enhanced it and brought it into the bluegrass realm.

When he joined Bill Monroe's Blue Grass Boys, Scruggs astounded all who watched and heard him. He could elicit from the banjo continuous rolls of notes, *arpeggios,* up and down the scale in a rapid barrage that transformed any tune, any break into his own and onto its own plane. In the context of the ensemble, with its fast picking, improvised solo instrumental breaks, the high, bluesy harmony vocals were matched nobly by Scruggs's banjo, sounding out the melody line as clearly as the fiddle. Banjo, specifically what is now referred to as "Scruggs style," was the final critical component of Bill Monroe's music, as yet unnamed but now undeniably distinctive.

Monroe's music began to set standards; the sound and style of presentation began to be copied widely, although it exhibited some regional variations. Personal appearances, recordings, and radio broadcasts propelled Bill Monroe and his Blue Grass Boys into the spotlight with their novel music that was no longer hillbilly, not really folk, and not quite the same as the country music current to the times. Bands began to emerge that took on the characteristics of Monroe's.

Within a period of a very few years, what erupted was not only an explosion of this vibrant new style of music but also variations that presented subtle differences. These fluctuations were inherent both in the repertoires and in the actual stage presentation.

A rough-edged, "mountain-style" variation was combined skillfully by Carter and Ralph Stanley, from southwest Virginia. Slightly younger contemporaries of Bill Monroe, they had a repertoire and singing style that drew from the simpler, more solemn ballads and traditions that imbued their mountain home community.

One such song, rendered a cappella and recently popularized by Ralph Stanley in *O Brother, Where Art Thou?,* is the haunting "O Death." The recurring theme song from that same film, "I Am a Man of Constant Sorrow," was handed down through oral tradition by the Stanley Brothers' father who would sing it to them during their childhood. The themes of such songs reflected the tough life, a never-ending battle against life's challenges and tribulations. The music was infused with deeply felt gospel inflections, testament to the faith instilled in area residents. Carter Stanley died in 1966, but Ralph has carried on since, accompanied by his Clinch Mountain Boys, the Stanley sound taking its place alongside the Monroe tradition.

A third distinct deviation of Monroe's music evolved when Lester Flatt and Earl Scruggs left Monroe's Blue Grass Boys in 1948 and went out on their own to form the Foggy Mountain Boys. Looking heavily to the Carter Family repertoire to draw from, the two chose the Carters' "Foggy Mountain Top" as the source of the band name. While Flatt and Scruggs took with them the core of Monroe's now distinctive musical style, Earl's banjo, their presentation, like that of the Stanley Brothers, developed its own flair. Flatt demonstrated an easy-going, natural elegance on stage as he handled the emcee work, something akin to a living room intimacy even in a big concert setting. They initially seldom featured mandolin in the group, instead opting later for the dobro, brought in when Josh Graves joined the group, and giving it a lead role alongside banjo and fiddle. Flatt's mellow voice with its special inflection was inviting; Scruggs's banjo work was enthralling.

To fully comprehend the subtle differences in bluegrass styles, one simply must listen to examples of each. It will not likely happen instantaneously or overnight, but the more you listen to a variety of artists, eventually a light bulb will go off in your head once you are able to perceive the nuances. It will help you to appreciate and understand the lines along which the music has developed, as well as those components that have remained unchanged.

BLUEGRASS: NOT YET IN THE DICTIONARY

As demonstrated, the "birth" of bluegrass music was a chronology and a combination of events. In spite of its formal birth with the addition of Scruggs-style banjo in Monroe's band providing the crowning moment, the naming of the "child" did not occur for a decade beyond that time. Monroe's music continued to be referred to in print and on stage varyingly as "folk music," "country," and still occasionally as "hillbilly," although this term was losing ground as we entered the 1950s.

Monroe, Flatt and Scruggs, the Stanleys, and numerous others had been making recordings through the years. However, the word *bluegrass* was not used in print until it appeared in the liner notes of what is now acknowledged as the first bluegrass album. Produced by Mike Seeger (folk icon Pete Seeger's half-brother), *American Banjo: Scruggs Style* was released in 1957. Musician and field researcher Ralph Rinzler provided the annotation, referring to the music associated with the Scruggs style of banjo picking as bluegrass. He was apparently following the lead of radio announcers and fans who had begun to informally call the music played by Monroe and his band, as well as that performed by other similar bands, "bluegrass."

A second album, *Mountain Music, Bluegrass Style*, released in 1959, again put the word bluegrass in print, further stamping it into the lexicon. Mike Seeger, in his liner notes to this recording, provided a concise but comprehensive overview of the music's makeup and history, the first time such a description had been set forth.

Bluegrass, as a separate and distinct genre, was given further credence and a special sense of respectability when in 1959 Alan Lomax wrote the article "Bluegrass Background: Folk Music with Overdrive" for *Esquire*. Here was a broader, more mainstream audience being addressed during the seedling days of the sixties' folk boom. Music then, just as today, often came with preconceived notions. Bluegrass, whether called by that term or not, still carried hillbilly, backwoods connotations, often impeding efforts to get good publicity or radio airplay.

Louise Scruggs, Earl's wife, was one of the first women to work behind the scenes in bluegrass, taking on the role in 1955 as manager and booking agent for Flatt and Scruggs. She recalled the following when I interviewed her in October 2002:

> The first time I heard it called bluegrass was 1958. I booked Earl and Flatt from 1955 up until their partnership stopped, and then he started Earl Scruggs Revue. But I never did book them in the capacity of the bluegrass act simply because radio stations would not play bluegrass. No bluegrass was played, really, all over the country. So I kept them, in their publicity [materials], in the country music field and they got a lot of airplay. Whenever they had a single released, it always got played. You couldn't get a bluegrass album or record played.

I went on to specifically ask if she *avoided* using the word *bluegrass*. Louise's emphatic response: "Absolutely. Called it country." This exemplifies the commercial climate at that time for bluegrass, a climate that persists today, with only small inroads being made in spite of its recent enormous successes. Nevertheless, commercial airplay or not, the music took hold, primarily kicked a notch higher with a big assist from the burgeoning folk boom as the sixties came into view.

While the instances mentioned are believed to be the earliest documented print references to the genre as "bluegrass," it remains unclear, or at least undocumented, as to whether Bill Monroe spoke of his own music as "bluegrass" in earlier years. However, as early as the mid-fifties, there are known references to his calling the music "bluegrass" in stage patter and in interviews.

Three such occurrences are recapped in Neil Rosenberg's book, *Bluegrass: A History*, relating to a trio of Monroe appearances. The earliest was an onstage inference at the New River Ranch in Rising Sun, Maryland, in May 1956 where Monroe thanked the promoter for supporting "bluegrass type of music." At the first full-day bluegrass event, on July 4, 1961, in Luray,

Virginia, Monroe made reference to "bluegrass people" as well as "bluegrass music" in on-stage comments. In 1965, at the Roanoke Bluegrass Festival in Fincastle, Virginia, the first weekend-long bluegrass festival, Monroe made mention of the Stanley Brothers "following in [his] footsteps" with "a bluegrass string band."

The Sullivan Family of Alabama is one of a handful of exclusively gospel bluegrass groups who have a long history in the music. Country star Marty Stuart got his start as a twelve-year-old, playing mandolin with the Sullivans. In their autobiographical book *The Sullivan Family: Fifty Years in Bluegrass Music, 1949–1999,* Enoch and Margie Sullivan recall hearing a *Grand Ole Opry Warm-Up Show* "some time in the mid-sixties," in which long-time *Opry* announcer Grant Turner was interviewing Bill Monroe prior to that night's appearance.

According to the Sullivans, they remember Monroe informing Turner that, from then on, he wanted "his" music to be called "bluegrass music." Turner, apparently not quite understanding the full intent of what Monroe was saying, tried to clarify that Monroe would still be performing "country" with his "Blue Grass Boys" from the "Bluegrass" state of Kentucky. The Sullivans recollect that Monroe went on to correct Turner, explaining that he wanted bluegrass to be "separate" from country due to his dissatisfaction over the direction country music was taking at that time. It is the Sullivans' contention, based on their memory of that exchange, that this is how and when Bill Monroe himself named the music and that Grant Turner honored Monroe's request from that night onward.[2]

When the word *bluegrass*, as it relates to the music, first appeared in standard dictionaries is also unclear and likely varied depending on the publishing house. A random check of dictionaries owned by family and friends, with copyrights ranging from 1958 to 1996, did not find the word *bluegrass* with its music definition until a 1988 *Webster's New World Dictionary of American English, Third College Edition.* Seven dictionaries consulted included various versions by Webster, Oxford, and Funk and Wagnalls; only 1988 and 1996 copyrighted books showed the definition. However, a detailed entry is provided in the supplement to the 1975 *Dictionary of American Slang, Second Supplemented Edition.* This clearly exemplifies how very young bluegrass is in terms of popular culture, truly a twentieth-century creation.[3]

[2] *The Sullivan Family: Fifty Years in Bluegrass Music, 1949–1999,* by Enoch and Margie Sullivan with Robert Gentry (Sweet Dreams Publishing Co., Many, Louisiana), http://thesullivanfly.com/book/bill_monroe.htm.

[3] It is not definitively known why Monroe named his band using two words versus "bluegrass"; the term usually is found as one word in dictionaries referencing the type of lawn grass as well as the state nickname. It has been commonly accepted that the music is known as one word, while Monroe's sidemen remain his "Blue Grass Boys."

THE BLUEGRASS FAMILY TREE GROWS

As artists continued to gain recognition, the touring circuit widened, exposing new audiences to the still developing genre. The bluegrass family tree was spreading. Performing groups were taking on a polish in their stage presence; instrumental virtuosity was keener and cleaner and more individualistic within the basic parameters of the music. With variety and musical infusions, bluegrass began to be shaped and further defined by its players.

But it was still in its first generation. Many of its artists had been former (or would be future) Blue Grass Boys; others had been members of other established or up-and-coming bands originally seen as country, transforming into being called bluegrass. Some were only children when first mesmerized by their earliest experiences hearing or seeing live bluegrass.

It is often noted that one of the best training grounds in bluegrass was to have been a member of Bill Monroe's Blue Grass Boys. By the time Monroe died in 1996, some one hundred twenty-five to two hundred musicians had passed through his "school." There are no precise records; some players can boast having played a single date with Monroe, while others had relatively long stints lasting a number of years.

Moreover, the Blue Grass Boys were not exclusively "boys." Bessie Lee Mauldin held up the bass post for several years, while Sally Ann Forrester played accordion. Accordion was featured occasionally in early country bands. Both women appear on Monroe recordings as well.

Changes in bluegrass band personnel are very common and generally not detrimental as one might expect. A major reason bluegrass remains a fresh, exciting music is the high turnover in bands. Almost a tradition in the music, it is like a never-ending school, musicians interning with one group, stepping up to the next and the next, until an artist often breaks away, forms, and leads his or her own band.

Time and again, the multitude of personnel changes that takes place in the majority of bluegrass bands even today points to two important aspects of bluegrass. The ensemble sound reflects the essence of bluegrass; it *is* bluegrass. And, second, band leaders continue to shape that ensemble sound to preserve the drive, the energy, the persona epitomized by their groups, simultaneously permitting them to breathe, expand, and continually cultivate new fans.

Here are just a handful of artists from the early years of bluegrass whose music I encourage you to explore further. Use them as a jumping off board to other artists with whom they worked or who passed through the ranks of their bands. Some, as you will discover, are still performing today, a testament to the durability of bluegrass and its artists. A number of those mentioned in the following paragraphs have traveled the path from first- to second-generation bluegrass and beyond. The next chapter will take you into those subsequent generations.

Among the artists whose styles or repertoires set them apart during the early years of bluegrass was Don Reno, who was Bill Monroe's next banjo player on Earl's exit. His banjo playing had a quality about it, too, that, while emphasizing the three-finger technique, presented the music with shades of "modern" country, hinting at the rockabilly era not yet formed but about to descend. His jazzy syncopation was in many respects reminiscent of Scott Joplin ragtime, filled with full chords and overfilled (tastefully) with notes. His exceptional guitar-playing abilities likely contributed to his novel approach on banjo.

Reno went on to form the Tennessee Cut-Ups with rhythm guitar ace Red Smiley; their numerous recordings made in a relatively short period in the early fifties facilitated the group's success while propelling the music into a wider commercial realm. Reno later teamed with extraordinary vocalist Bill Harrell. Music of the Reno family has continued, primarily under the baton of son Ronnie, who played mandolin and sang with his father at the age of ten. Today he carries on Don's music and legacy as Ronnie Reno and the Reno Tradition.

One of the most colorful figures in bluegrass is Jimmy Martin. It is debatable as to which is more overpowering, his incredibly forthright vocals or his often loudly patterned suit jackets. As a member of Bill Monroe's Blue Grass Boys after Flatt's departure, Martin is noted for placing, in a complementary match to Monroe's voice, the "high lonesome sound" as a permanent marker of bluegrass. "Widow Maker," "Sunny Side of the Mountain," and "Freeborn Man" are among his numerous memorable hits, so many of which are staples of the bluegrass repertoire. An exceptional showman whose band style permeated contemporary bluegrass and remains a model, he has led the Sunny Mountain Boys since the mid-1950s.

Here, too, is another example of "Boys" not being exclusively male. For many years beginning in 1968, Gloria Belle Flickinger sang lead and played bass for Martin. She later worked with Charlie Monroe for a brief period. Today she performs as Gloria Belle and Tennessee Sunshine.

A key figure to come out of one of Jimmy Martin's lineups is innovative banjo player J.D. Crowe, whose impeccable timing and considerable drive are flawless. As a musician who guided many "second-generation" bluegrass artists, Crowe introduced legions of new audiences to banjo and bluegrass via his rock-and-blues-infused music that he developed with his group in the late sixties, J.D. Crowe and the New South.

Another central figure is Mac Wiseman, whose expressive singing remains one of the most distinctive in the genre. He, too, is a Blue Grass Boy alumnus and was in the original lineup of the Flatt and Scruggs band. His "voice with a heart," as so many have called it, is permanently engraved in bluegrass history on the classic cut with Bill Monroe of "Can't You Hear Me Callin'," one of Monroe's final Columbia label efforts. He has enjoyed great success working in both bluegrass and country music, recording a wide range of material, including one of his biggest hits, the Carter Family's "Jimmy Brown the Newsboy."

Other innovators of that first generation of bluegrass included Jim and Jesse and the Virginia Boys. The close McReynolds brothers' harmonies were often compared to that of the country-pop Everly Brothers. Jesse's unusual mandolin technique set the stage for a generation of mandolinists who have since followed.

Jim and Jesse brought traditional bluegrass to a wider circle of new fans as their repertoire crossed generations and genres. Making their recording debut in 1952, they incorporated such classic material as Louvin Brothers' songs (e.g., "Are You Missing Me?") alongside country, folk, and pop. It is their version of contemporary songwriter John Prine's "Paradise," about the coal-mining town, that most people recognize.

Here, again, is a group that demonstrates clearly the family connection prevalent in bluegrass. Jim and Jesse's grandfather, Charles McReynolds, was one of the first to record for RCA Victor in Bristol in 1927. Until the effects of multiple sclerosis forced him to quit, Jesse's son, Keith, was for many years their bass player. Moreover, although brother Jim passed away December 31, 2002, Jesse continues to carry on the family tradition. His grandson, Luke McKnight, who joined the Virginia Boys in 1997 at age fifteen, has stepped into the spotlight alongside him.

In the 1940s, Carl Story began to carve his niche in the music. He was a multi-instrumentalist who played fiddle for Monroe for a brief period. He went on to establish himself in the forefront of bluegrass gospel, hence, his moniker as the "Father of Bluegrass Gospel." Story particularly gained notoriety with his sidemen, the Rambling Mountaineers, when the genre came of age in the fifties.

Everett and "Bea," the Lilly Brothers, were originally from West Virginia, where they had been regulars on WWVA's *Wheeling Jamboree*. Everett, for a time, worked with Flatt and Scruggs. Fiddling Tex Logan, who had been a sideman with Wilma Lee and Stoney Cooper (discussed later), had gone to MIT in Boston in the very early fifties to complete his graduate studies. There, he was instrumental in convincing the Lilly Brothers to move to the area, where they, along with a phenomenal banjo player, Don Stover, helped inspire and influence a previously untapped wellspring for bluegrass in New England.

Logan, who worked with Bill Monroe on occasion, is known not only for his exciting fiddle playing, but also for his songwriting. Two songs in particular, "Diamond Joe," first popularized by the Coopers, and "Christmas Time's a-Comin'" for Monroe, have been recorded widely. Emmylou Harris's rendition of the latter can often be heard on department store music systems during the holiday season.

Mentioned earlier, the Sullivan Family was an early gospel bluegrass group, which emerged as the 1950s began. Their presentations, infused with emotion, in part have relied on such gospel music songs as those from the Louvin Brothers and the Bailes Brothers.

The Bailes Brothers made a name for themselves in the early years of country with their close brother harmonies. They appeared regularly on the *Opry* and developed a large repertory of material, focusing on gospel. Their "Dust on the Bible" and "Give Mother My Crown," among numerous others, have been widely recorded within bluegrass. The Bailes Brothers were also co-founders of the *Louisiana Hayride* radio program in Shreveport, Louisiana.

Perhaps the most riveting and entertaining gospel bluegrass ensemble that endures today is the Lewis Family. Roy "Pop" Lewis, Sr. and his young bride, Pauline Holloway, eloped in 1925. In the 1940s, along with half of their eight children, they formed their singing group. Over the years, they became identified as the "First Family of Bluegrass Gospel," with a classic show-business bent to their performances, straight out of vaudeville. Children, their spouses, and grandchildren have passed through the group's gates at varying times.

"Little Roy" Lewis remains the unmistakable centerpiece. With a knack for offbeat humor, he is a virtuosic multi-instrumentalist. His prowess on the five-string banjo is matched on guitar, autoharp, and upright bass, to name a few. His notorious penchant for popping in on stage during other performers' sets, usually in a silly costume, is proof positive, time and again, what troupers bluegrass musicians are; the targets of Little Roy's antics rarely miss a beat in spite of the belly laughs that he incites.

On a serious note, the rousing vocal harmonies put across by Little Roy and his sisters, Polly, Miggie, and Janis, and other relatives who fill out the multigenerational group, are exceptional. A lot of their material draws from the writing of Randall Hylton, who was one of the best bluegrass songwriters in the genre. His "Slippers with Wings" is one of their most beloved numbers.

Young Lewis Family members often take to the stage before they are old enough to start grade school, as was the case with Lewis Phillips, Janis's son, who debuted on banjo at age five. Senior status is no deterrent either. Until five years prior to her death in 2003, matriarch "Mom" Lewis would travel with the family and staff the merchandise table. "Pop" Lewis, born in 1905, toured and performed regularly until 2000, when surgery kept his touring to a minimum. His last public performance was May 2, 2003, at the Lewis Family's 16th Annual Homecoming and Bluegrass Festival, held near their homeplace of Lincolnton, Georgia. "Pop" died less than a year later on March 23, 2004, at the age of ninety-eight.

One of the most commercially successful groups to come out of the early fifties' bluegrass period was Sonny and Bobby, the Osborne Brothers. With their feet planted firmly in tradition, both worked separately with some of the moving forces in bluegrass. A multi-instrumentalist whose high tenor vocals can crack fine leaded crystal, Bobby formed a short-lived band with

Jimmy Martin and worked with the Stanleys for a brief period before entering the service. Six years younger, Sonny landed a job playing banjo with
Bill Monroe at the ripe young age of fourteen.

Performing together as the Osborne Brothers since November 6, 1953,
Bobby and Sonny have brought a modern immediacy to bluegrass without
compromising its roots. Predecessors to the second generation of bluegrass,
when many different influences began to take hold, they injected a sparkling
energy into the music. Their repertoire, since their inception as a team, has
seamlessly blended old with new. The first song they ever recorded, "Ruby,
Are You Mad at Your Man?" from Depression-era singer Cousin Emmy, was
a crowd pleaser that has remained one of their signature songs.

The Osbornes have recorded extensively from the vast catalog of
husband-and-wife songwriting team Felice and Boudleaux Bryant, perhaps the most prolific composing team ever in country music. The Bryants
also wrote most of the hits for rock-and-roll's Everly Brothers. A Bryant
song, "Rocky Top," would take the Osborne Brothers to unprecedented
heights. They recorded the song and then released it on Christmas Day,
1967. It subsequently sold 85,000 copies by the first week in January.
Since then, "Rocky Top" has become one of the most recorded bluegrass
songs ever and has logged more than 1.2 million radio performances.[4]
In 1982, it was voted an official state song of Tennessee.

The Osborne Brothers truly were steppingstones as traditional bluegrass
segued its way into uncharted waters at the beginning of the folk boom.
Altering the placement of harmonies to *below* high tenor lead, they set a
new course for the bluegrass vocal sound. In addition, they went on to
break the barrier on electric instrumentation, "plugging in" and experi-
menting with such nonacoustic instruments as drums and pedal steel. They
also were the first bluegrass band to give a concert for a college audience
(1960), and they were the first bluegrass group ever to appear at the White
House (1973).

Significant within the history of the Osborne Brothers was a relatively
short-lived association with singer-guitarist Harley "Red" Allen. As a trio,
they recorded a handful of sides for MGM from 1955 to 1958, producing a modest hit with "Once More," the same song that paved the way
for the novel harmonies noted earlier. Later, Allen's razor-sharp distinctive voice was captured on recordings made in the sixties with the unusual
mandolinist Frank Wakefield. Recently rereleased by Rebel Records, these
classic cuts, among those made with other seminal players, represent an
important chapter in the development and acceptance of bluegrass during
the folk era.

[4]As of April 6, 2004, according to statistics provided by Broadcast Music, Inc.
(BMI).

NOT JUST BLUEGRASS "BOYS"

Although not prominent, women were making their presence felt early on in the evolving bluegrass realm. This changed significantly in the 1980s, during which time more women took on lead roles in bands. Placed within social and historical perspective, the fact that women did not typically pursue leadership situations within the music is not surprising or unusual. Few women in other music categories had done so either.

The social agenda of the era, along with the fact that many of these first, defining groups came from rural farm regions, coal-mining communities, and textile industry towns, precluded most women from the desire or ability to leave a family and tour with a music group. These were not times when women just picked up and went out on the road. Families had to be looked after, so women, even if they could pick or dance, would stay home and do so. Music making for them was largely reserved for family celebrations and social gatherings or evening relaxation on the back porch.

Evidence points to some men in bluegrass being resistant to women coming on board or leading bands, even post–women's liberation movement years. This scenario, while true, still has to be placed in context of the times. Changing attitudes is a process, one that continues today. The percentage of women active full-time in bluegrass appears to be increasing as bluegrass makes strides in popularity.

Nevertheless, women have certainly left their mark in bluegrass and old-time country music. As discussed in chapter 2, cousins Sara and Maybelle Carter were primary movers behind early country and from whose repertoire many genres, including bluegrass, have borrowed. Numerous others, either on their own or within family groups, have been among the most remarkable.

The prolific country music family of Ernest V. "Pop" and Hattie Stoneman had already tasted considerable success in earlier decades with their best-selling "The Sinking of the Titanic"; they gained a new and renewed following with the emergence of the bluegrass sound in the late forties.

Recognizing the commercial potential of traditional music, they had carved a career out of their southern Appalachian heritage. Over the years, along with their many children, they performed at varying times as the Stoneman Family or the Bluegrass Champs, moving handily in and out of bluegrass and country to meet the trends, including hosting their own syndicated television program in the sixties.

Youngest daughter, Roni, was the first woman ever to record bluegrass banjo; she appears as Veronica Stoneman Cox on the important *American Banjo: Scruggs Style* album mentioned earlier. Roni went on to great success as a regular for twenty years on television's *Hee Haw*, portraying the comic character "Ida Lee Nagger" as well as picking banjo. A seasoned entertainer,

she continues today to wow audiences with expert musicianship, accompanied by her down-home humor. In Roni's newest bluegrass band, sister
Donna occasionally sits in on mandolin.

Among the children, Scotty Stoneman also gained a considerable repu-
tation for his fiery fiddle playing, which won him several national championship titles. His incredible command of his instrument can be heard on
recently reissued recordings by the legendary Kentucky Colonels.

One of the most vibrant women of bluegrass is Wilma Lee Cooper, who,
performing with fiddle-playing husband Stoney, walked both sides of the
genre line with the second foot in country. Popular artists on the *Wheeling
Jamboree* in West Virginia, the two were a strikingly handsome couple whose
professionalism and genuine warmth endeared them to fans. They were one
of the first to feature dobro as a mainstay instrument. Wilma Lee's renditions of traditional ballads and gospel songs, such as "Poor Ellen Smith" and
"Bury Me Beneath the Willow," are among the most memorable.

After Stoney's death in 1977, Wilma Lee continued to lead her Clinch
Mountain Clan, whose members featured superb players. Among them were
dobroist Gene Wooten, who was a much sought-after studio musician; banjo
trendsetter Butch Robins, a former Blue Grass Boy; and bass player Terry
Smith, more recently a member of the Osborne Brothers' band. Terry and
his brother Billy are two of Nashville's most popular songwriters. Always
energetic and active, Wilma Lee, a regular on the *Grand Ole Opry*, was side-
lined by a stroke and made her final appearance there March 21, 2001.

Two women, among countless others, whose significance cannot be overlooked, rose up from the early years. Their impact continues to be felt in
the music of younger generations. Molly O'Day was destined for stardom,
with a commanding voice and banjo playing to match. Her career spanned
the 1940s and essentially ended in 1952. In late 1946, she recorded several
songs, among others, written by Hank Williams, but turned to religion and
gospel music to which she devoted herself for the rest of her life. Among
her admirers are country stars Dolly Parton and Patty Loveless, both of
whom have turned to bluegrass on recent recordings. Both exhibit punch
in their vocals similar to that of O'Day's.

Rose Maddox enjoyed notoriety performing country music with her
brothers, first on local radio, starting at the age of eleven, later gaining great
success on such programs as the *Louisiana Hayride* and the *Grand Ole Opry*.
She and her brothers were also trendsetters, establishing the flashy "cowboy"
style of stage dress that remains popular with many acts even today.

Maddox had a magnificent voice and delivery. Instrumental in the furtherance of honky-tonk and rockabilly, she is also remembered for pairing
with country great Buck Owens. However, her place in the history of bluegrass was secured when Rose embraced the music and became the first
woman to record a bluegrass album. With assistance on the recording from
Bill Monroe, Don Reno, and Red Smiley, in 1962 she released to great

acclaim *Rose Maddox Sings Bluegrass*. Maddox remained faithful to bluegrass with her inimitable vocal style until her death in 1998. Her legacy was especially felt on the West Coast where women musicians seemed to flourish, particularly from the mid-seventies on, and where bluegrass itself developed distinctive regional stylistics.

Women continued to contribute to the growth of bluegrass as the 1950s progressed and the sixties folk era converged. Banjo player Murphy Henry writes regularly and exclusively about women in bluegrass in her quarterly newsletter (see "Where to from Here"). As this book went to press, she was preparing the first full-length manuscript devoted to the women of bluegrass.

THE BALLAD OF EARL SCRUGGS

Earl Scruggs hails originally from the community of Flint Hill near Shelby, North Carolina. Born in 1924, Scruggs grew up in a region rich in banjo players. He set the world on fire with his brand of banjo picking when he joined Bill Monroe and his Blue Grass Boys and continued that spark as partner to Lester Flatt. With Flatt, their music became embedded in American popular culture with "The Ballad of Jed Clampett," the theme song for the 1960s television show, *The Beverly Hillbillies*. A reprise of their "Foggy Mountain Breakdown" in the movie *Bonnie and Clyde* reinforced it.

Years later, with the formation of his Earl Scruggs Revue, Earl continued—as he still does—to set standards, providing new outlets for the sound of banjo with innovative explorations of and collaborations with all types of music. On February 13, 2003, he became the first banjo player to receive a star on the Hollywood Walk of Fame.

SPL: You were an innovator within a tradition by taking the banjo and popularizing a particular playing style. Into the eighties, you continued to be an innovator, breaking out of the bonds of bluegrass and expanding on the music in a variety of directions, from bluegrass to rock-and-roll to blues. In addition, you have recorded with everyone from the Chieftains to Billy Joel. To what do you attribute your open-mindedness to other forms of music?

ES: I've never wanted to be penned into just one category. I like straight bluegrass music, but I also think the banjo can fit in with other types of music as well. I've proven that over the years working with the [Earl Scruggs] Revue, which was my sons. I still have [my son] Gary with me playing bass.

SPL: What or whose music influenced you early on?

ES: When I first started, there weren't any other banjo pickers that pick like I do. I wondered for weeks and weeks before I went into the business how, if at all, I would be accepted into the music.

When I went to the *Grand Ole Opry* in 1945, they had two banjo pickers there. One was Uncle Dave Macon and the other one was Stringbean. It just seemed that the banjo, the style that I played, turned Bill Monroe's music into, well, the banjo [became] a full member of the band. [For example] I could play the slow tunes as well as the up-tempo tunes.

SPL: If you could play only one song on the banjo for a group of people who had never before heard bluegrass, what song would it be, and why would you choose it to represent bluegrass?

ES: I guess it would have to be "Foggy Mountain Breakdown." It's so simple. I don't want to say that people like just a simple tune, but it's one that I think you could hum, and it'd be pretty, a time or two. I know it worked for me and, if I could hum a tune, it's almost a hit in my mind. The "Foggy Mountain Breakdown" is a tune [that's] easy to hum along with.

SPL: What has been the most rewarding aspect of bringing the banjo and bluegrass to a worldwide audience?

ES: That's an impossible question to answer, I guess. I will say that, as long as I've been in the business, well, all forms of music, as well as bluegrass, have their peaks and valleys. Somebody'll come along with a hit tune and it'll just skyrocket that particular type of music for awhile. Then somebody will come along and have a fresh sound. But bluegrass, when I went in it to work in 1945, it wasn't really established into its own category of music, but I think the banjo put it into a bluegrass category.

SPL: What do you look for in a great-sounding banjo?

ES: Of course, they have to have quite a bit of volume. Now, with all the help of sound systems and good microphones, you [don't] need so much volume. My banjo has a mellow tone to it. Some banjos will get to sounding a little too brassy. I think the reason for that is they might put a little too much metal into the instrument itself. You can go to a certain limit with metal, but you have to tone it down a little bit with some good wood also.

SPL: How do you preserve the tradition of the music while expanding on it to reach others outside the bluegrass tradition?

(*Without hesitation, Scruggs offered his answer almost before the question was asked.*)

ES: I never give it a thought; I just play what feels good to me and hopefully people will like it. If they don't, that's their problem. But I'm just not a-going to stay with a certain sound all my life, 'cause I'm not on earth long enough to pass up a good opportunity (*laughing*). So I'm going to play all kinds of music, as long as it's good, respectable music.

SPL: Could there be bluegrass without banjo?

ES: We would have to experience it to really answer that. I think the banjo really fit in, what made it become a type of music of its own. But I don't want to sound like I was the one that started it, because I was the first one to play what is now called "bluegrass" banjo or "Earl Scruggs–style" banjo pickin'. There have been so many other good banjo pickers that have come along. The world's full of good banjo pickers now, thank goodness.

Interview conducted October 24, 2002, Count Basie Theatre, Red Bank, New Jersey.

4

Bluegrass Bends and Blends

The family tree of bluegrass is more like a forest of tangled roots and branches. As discussed in preceding chapters, its origins run deep and wide. Even after bluegrass emerged a distinct genre, almost immediately subtle variations were seen and heard. The music was heading into its second and subsequent generations.

A mere decade after its birth, differences began to take hold that redrew the boundaries of bluegrass. Styles developed that some would continue to identify as bluegrass, while others would call them progressive, newgrass, and new acoustic. Hard-core traditionalists would go so far as to opine, "That's not bluegrass," especially when an electric bass appeared on stage. Then blends developed, marrying bluegrass with jazz, classical, rock, and ethnic genres.

By all accounts, the changes that occurred in the late fifties and through-out the sixties caused the music to proliferate. The folk boom heavily fueled these conditions. With a diversity of approaches to bluegrass came a naturally expanded audience.

Some of the variations that occurred corresponded to particular geo-graphic centers of activity. At the same time, the bending and blending of bluegrass did not impede the start-up of new *traditional* bluegrass groups alongside these branches; in fact, both camps have continued to surface and thrive right up through present day. Furthermore, newly composed "tradi-tion" songs were, and still are, being added to the pioneers' repertory.

The exposure triggered by the folk era gave bluegrass one of its biggest early pushes into public view, setting the stage for its viability in situations other than intimate concerts or informal jam sessions. The bluegrass festival as an "event" emerged in the mid-sixties as did the first print publication, *Bluegrass Unlimited*, devoted to the music.

During these still formative years, different schools of bluegrass developed in such urban locales as the greater New York area, Boston, Washington, D.C., and its surrounds, and on the West Coast in San Francisco and Los Angeles, to name a few. Certainly, the Tennessee-Kentucky-Virginia-North Carolina region, among others, continued to produce a multitude of musicians who did not always remain within the strictly traditional Monroe idiom.

The ever-growing complexity of bluegrass was, and still is, reflected within its often-nuanced diversity as each new square on the multipatterned quilt of bluegrass has been added. Just as Elvis, the Beatles, Springsteen, Sting, and Kiss broke barriers with their brands of rock-and-roll, so have any number of second-, third-, and fourth-generation bluegrass artists.

Branches continue to grow as artists' careers span multiple generations and as many perpetuate a bluegrass family name in the business. Some musicians who stepped into leadership roles in the 1960s or 1970s interned with established groups in the late forties and into the next decade. Those coming into the limelight today, at the helm of top-selling bands, came up through the ranks of second- and third-generation bluegrass.

ROOTS REVISITED

To understand how changes infiltrated bluegrass during its second generation, one must revisit the roots of bluegrass. Sometimes roots can be so long and extensive that they reappear in unanticipated places. For bluegrass, its roots were vital to a huge growth spurt more than a decade after it first came barreling onto the music scene.

Ola Belle Reed and Jean Ritchie are two crossover artists whose music stemmed from family traditions nurtured during the first half of the twentieth century but whose influence was felt in bluegrass primarily during the second half. Their contributions continue to impact and to be relevant, and make for excellent examples here.

Best known in old-time music circles, Ola Belle Reed took the traditional ballads of her native North Carolina and introduced them to new audiences north of the Mason-Dixon Line. Along with her brother, Alec Campbell, and husband, Ralph "Bud" Reed, Ola Belle established a music park, the New River Ranch, in Rising Sun, Maryland, which they operated from 1951 until 1957 and where they presented traditional music concerts and performed as Ola Belle's New River Boys. Two to three years later, they became the "home band" across the state line at Sunset Park near West Grove, Pennsylvania, where they appeared for the next two decades. Genres mixed freely without categorization; it was an era during which bluegrass began to flourish because of these open doors.

Not only did Ola Belle render the old songs in her inimitable style, frailing banjo to accompany herself, but she also wrote songs that would be adopted as anthems by many. One such song, "High on a Mountain," has been given numerous treatments, most notably by bluegrass band leader Del McCoury, who transformed it into a bluegrass standard recorded by many since his 1972 cut. Country superstar Marty Stuart, who throughout his career has demonstrated respect for his musical roots, took the song to new heights with his soulful hit version in the early 1990s. Ola Belle Reed continued to perform until 1987 when she suffered a stroke; she passed away in 2002.

Jean Ritchie's story and legacy are similar to that of Ola Belle Reed's. Born in 1922, she has taken the music of her homeplace around the world, touching many with her gentle, but spirited, interpretations. The music was handed down by oral tradition to Jean and her siblings while growing up in Kentucky. During 1952 and 1953, on a Fulbright scholarship, Jean spent a year studying and researching in Ireland and the British Isles, the origin of her ancestors as well as the traditional music she performs.

As a folk artist, she laid important groundwork during the fifties and sixties for the furtherance of folk, bluegrass, and what many now refer to as "roots" music. Jean's renditions of traditional ballads sung a cappella or accompanying herself on her trademark mountain dulcimer, as well as her own compositions, have become staples in many folk songbooks. They have entwined themselves irrevocably into the bluegrass mix as well.

One example is her original "The L&N Don't Stop Here Anymore," about the declining coal-mining scene in Kentucky. It has been recorded by a diverse range of artists, from bluegrass music's New Coon Creek Girls to country's Johnny and June Carter Cash to contemporary folk stylist Michelle Shocked. "My Dear Companion" was included on the all-acoustic, bluegrass-flavored 1987 *Trio* album by Linda Ronstadt, Dolly Parton, and Emmylou Harris.

Traditional ballads and songs portrayed by Reed, Ritchie, and other roots artists of the time became folk music to a new generation; much of this, in turn, became source material for bluegrass musicians. In looking at such artists and their contributions, one need only recall that Bill Monroe adopted and adapted many elements of these same roots songs and tunes. Most of his "new" bluegrass music was, in reality, entrenched in the "old."

FOLK MEETS BLUEGRASS

The majority of changes that began to take place within bluegrass in the late fifties and throughout the sixties were not ones that altered the key features. Most involved differences in repertoire and in arrangements. Over time, however, some groups began to substitute electric bass for acoustic, and, on the heels of that, "other genre" explorations took bluegrass into more divergent directions.

Reaching back into the old-time catalog of traditional songs and tunes served to bridge the sociocultural divide for the still young bluegrass music. With the phenomenon of the folk boom unfolding, college students and larger numbers of professionals began to take notice, taking bluegrass further into urban circles where it was still just beginning to pierce.

The springboard, in part, was old-time music, "authentic folk" in the eyes of academia, as explained in chapter 1. Old-time music, until about the mid- to late seventies, was almost exclusively drawn from oral tradition, thereby giving it validity or credence in these disciplines. With entrée via old-time proponents, the doors to bluegrass swung open. Folk revivalists provided the big push through those doors.

Folk revivalists are those with an interest in a particular authentic, older style and who embrace it, learn it, and go on to perform it, usually with the intent of earning a living doing so. Not only do such practitioners take traditional ballads and folksongs and re-create them, they often write new songs "in the tradition," that is, that sound old and authentic.

There were a number of key people instrumental in the merging of old with new, introducing bluegrass into the evolving tapestry of popular folk music. One was Bill Clifton, born to a prominent Baltimore family and raised on a farm in the Maryland countryside. With an avid interest in old-time country and folk music, he began his music career in the early fifties, recording and touring solo as well as with many other established artists, carrying bluegrass around the world. In the mid-fifties, he also published a widely circulated folk songbook that served as a source of tunes for many bluegrass performers.

In addition, he made a major contribution to bluegrass when he organized the first full-day bluegrass event in Luray, Virginia, in 1961; this was the forerunner of multiday bluegrass festivals. He also was one of the coordinators for the then freshly reorganized and restarted Newport Folk Festival in 1963, where bluegrass received enormous exposure in its early years. Clifton continues to champion bluegrass and traditional music; in 2001, he released a retrospective boxed set of more than two hundred songs steeped in bluegrass and early country tradition.

The New Lost City Ramblers were integral to bluegrass's coming to the fore during the folk era. As musicians, John Cohen, Mike Seeger, and Tom Paley, later replaced by Tracy Schwarz, introduced thousands to old-time music, drawing from the wealth of authentic material and playing with masterful knowledge. They also brought in concert to city folk the performers whose music they reproduced. Cohen cofounded the Friends of Old Time Music, which served as the conduit that introduced New York City audiences to such traditional artists as legendary flatpicking guitarist Doc Watson, bluesman Mississippi John Hurt, and "Father of Bluegrass" Bill Monroe, as well as the Stanley Brothers.

Such exchanges of music permitted bluegrass to seep into the folk stream and, ultimately, into the public consciousness. All this served as preliminary to the further changes that took place and which can be attributed directly to the influence of what became popular folk music of that period.

John Cohen must be recognized for an additional contribution. An acclaimed photographer and filmmaker, Cohen was the first to coin the term *high lonesome sound*. In a mid-sixties' documentary he made about Kentucky traditional singer Roscoe Holcomb, he used the phrase to describe Holcomb's music; that description is now typically associated with the distinguishing qualities of the bluegrass vocal sound.

Out of the suburban Washington, D.C.-Maryland-northern Virginia area came a group that took advantage of older tunes being adapted by the new "folkies," adding them to a repertoire that already contained Monroe's music. The Country Gentlemen was founded in 1957 and is considered the group that initiated the progressive bluegrass movement.

The folklike, smooth bluegrass sound was established with the Country Gentlemen's first album, *Country Songs, Old and New*, released in 1960 on the heels of the publication in *Esquire* of the 1959 Lomax article about bluegrass. The album contained numerous traditional ballads, such as "The Little Sparrow," "Weeping Willow," and "Ellen Smith," all executed bluegrass style, replete with stunning harmonies, crisp banjo, and smart mandolin work. It was bluegrass, but it was not a typical array of bluegrass material. The banjo and mandolin had a bounce about their delivery that was askew to Scruggs and Monroe picking. Then again, some tunes exhibited straight-ahead, "in the tradition" bluegrass drive, such as in "Tomorrow's My Wedding Day." In addition, there was a hauntingly lilting, harmonized rendition of "The Long Black Veil," a hit the previous year for popular country singer Lefty Frizzell. Joan Baez would later embrace the Gents' version for her recording of the same song.

A short time after the release of this LP (i.e., vinyl recording), there was a change in bass players. Now the quartet was comprised of two extraordinary lead vocalists, guitarist Charlie Waller and John Duffey, who played mandolin and dobro. They were joined by cutting-edge banjo player–guitarist Eddie Adcock, a former Blue Grass Boy, who, while in the Gents, helped set the standard in bluegrass for baritone singing, and on upright bass, Tom Gray, whose novel "walking" technique countered the melody while providing a rhythm backup line. This configuration came to be known as the "Classic Country Gentlemen" and remained together, as is, for about four years.

This group promptly went back into the studio to record *Folk Songs and Bluegrass*, again turning to a rich storehouse of traditional songs, transformed into bluegrass by their folk-oriented interpretations. A combination of the repertoire and this lineup of the Country Gentlemen marked a turning point for the music, both in sound and in scope, setting in motion the progressive movement.

While the music of the "Gents" would create controversy, it also cultivated an expanded fan base. From here, bluegrass developed along a number of lines, all rooted similarly in the Monroe tradition but deviating, as mentioned earlier, with more eclectic repertoires, contemporary arrangements, or use of such instruments as electric bass or even an occasional percussion instrument.

A major trendsetting group grew out of the Country Gentlemen and in the same backyard. In 1971 in D.C., Duffey and Gray founded the Seldom Scene. Less limited in repertoire than even the permissive catalog that the Country Gentlemen looked to, the Scene drew from rock and other popular music as readily as it did from traditional and contemporarily written bluegrass. Their interpretation of J.J. Cale's "After Midnight" remains something of a cult classic.

Instrumentation was novel, too. Mike Auldridge brought dobro to the quintet, substituting for fiddle. Guitarist John Starling and banjo player Ben Eldridge filled out the group. The sophistication of their musical arrangements proved fruitful, attracting a wider age range of fans. The group became mainstays of the area, with standing gigs at area clubs, including the Birchmere in Alexandria, Virginia. The Seldom Scene endures today with Eldridge the only remaining original member, while Charlie Waller still guides the Country Gentlemen.

New York City's Greenwich Village, boosted by the folk boom of the late fifties and early sixties, served as a critical catalyst for bluegrass. Sing-alongs and jam sessions were abundant in Washington Square Park on the Village's north side. Budding bluegrassers mingled with such soon-to-be household names as Bob Dylan, Joan Baez, and Peter, Paul and Mary.

Perceptively riding on the coattails of the burgeoning folk scene, the Greenbriar Boys formed in the late 1950s. Their repertoire was an informed urban blend of bluegrass, old-time, and folk, and their high-energy presentations caught the attention of such artists as Joan Baez, with whom they recorded and toured. The Greenbriar Boys' visibility and acceptance during these years was a major advancement for bluegrass, garnering it recognition in more commercial realms.

Mandolinist for the Greenbriar Boys during much of this period was Ralph Rinzler. Rinzler's significance in bluegrass beyond this group cannot be overemphasized. Judiciously using the folk boom as a spark, he was responsible for rekindling Bill Monroe's career as well as for discovering Doc Watson, one of the most important multigenre guitarists of all times. Rinzler's savvy contributed heavily over the course of several decades to the furtherance of traditional music on many fronts, including several years spent as director of the influential Newport Folk Festival. In 1967, he founded and was director of the Smithsonian's Festival of the American Folklife (now called the Smithsonian Folklife Festival), which he headed until his death in 1994.

ALL THAT JAZZ AND . . .

The terms *progressive bluegrass*, *newgrass*, and *new acoustic* are often used interchangeably; however, this can be subjective. All refer to variations in bluegrass that involved one or more changes to the traditional sound and repertoire, including introduction of other genre influences, such as rock or jazz, use of electric or percussion instruments, and reliance upon contemporarily written songs that incorporated either of the first two.

The New York area produced many progressive bluegrass and newgrass groups as the years rolled into the seventies, each putting its own special stamp on the sound. From upstate New York came Country Cooking, a futuristic band that turned out not one but two of today's leading-edge banjo players, Pete Wernick and Tony Trischka.

Wernick, whose novel use of playing through a phase shifter[1] has become his trademark, went on to form Hot Rize in 1978. One of the most popular modern bluegrass groups ever, Hot Rize discontinued working together full-time in 1990 to pursue individual activities, accepting only select dates. Wernick continues breaking down barriers between genres, performing with his wife, Joan, also formerly of Country Cooking, as well as with his "bluegrass blend" band, Pete Wernick's Live Five, artfully combining Dixieland jazz-swing with bluegrass.

Trischka has since worked in numerous settings. His credits range from Broadway to made-for-television movies to commercial jingles. He has worked with alternative rock groups R.E.M. and Violent Femmes, as well. His group, Skyline, was a seminal East Coast group in the eighties, which relied heavily on original compositions and whose impact as an urban bluegrass ensemble was significant. With his latest Tony Trischka Band, he continues to stretch his inventiveness and to explore the nonboundaries of bluegrass, delving into jazz, classical, world music, rock, and blues.

New York State made another considerable contribution to bluegrass with the formation of the music's first all-women band in 1974. The Buffalo Gals, whose repertoire embraced bluegrass standards, pop-rock, swing, and more, stayed together only until 1979, but they led the way for more women to step into lead roles as well as to establish other exclusively female groups. Among the all-female bands who followed were the New Coon Creek Girls, Petticoat Junction, as well as country's Dixie Chicks, who started out in 1989 as a progressive bluegrass quartet.

Boston and its surrounds, already enjoying the talents of the Lilly Brothers, Don Stover, Tex Logan, and Joe Val since the early fifties, continued to attract creative musicians. Among those stomping the bluegrass ground in Harvard's back yard were Peter Rowan and Bill "Brad" Keith, who would not only become Blue Grass Boys but who would also contribute tremendously to the newgrass sound.

Rowan is a maverick who has never pigeonholed what he produces. His original music has woven bluegrass with strands of rock, Tex-Mex, Native

---

[1]A phase shifter is an electronic filtering device that creates the impression of the sound "coming and going."

American, reggae, and other ethnic forms. He was an important figure in several bluegrass "hybrid" groups that emerged on the West Coast and continues to explore many options.

Bill Keith put a new spin on Scruggs-style banjo playing that permitted note-for-note playing of complex fiddle tunes. He, too, can be found today with his musical hands in any number of activities.

Northern Lights is a New England–based contemporary bluegrass band whose origins go back to the mid-seventies. Its powerhouse sound earmarked a turning point for New England bluegrass in the 1980s. "Jazz-grass" banjo stylist and Compass Records founder Alison Brown passed through its ranks while attending Harvard University.

Also active in Bean Town in the seventies was the group Tasty Licks, a wellspring for several luminaries-to-be. Two were Pat Enright and Béla Fleck. Enright went on to cofound in 1984 the enduring Nashville Bluegrass Band. Internationally renowned in bluegrass and jazz communities alike, Fleck is today the world's best-known banjo interpreter.

While Fleck's development as a bender and blender of bluegrass began with forays into bebop while still in high school, it was with the pacesetting New Grass Revival in the eighties that his energies soared to higher elevations. When Fleck joined the band in 1982, it had been around for about a decade. Its already established sound had a heavy rock inflection, with extended, lengthy solo breaks and explosive "chops" such as those rendered on fiddle and mandolin by Sam Bush, a founding member. "Newgrass" was an apt designation. In addition to Bush and Fleck, the 1982 lineup consisted of John Cowan, whose dynamic blues vocals could carry to the next county, and guitarist Pat Flynn, whose slick jazz licks provided still another novel twist. Cowan's electric bass was joined by the others' acoustic instruments boosted via electric pickups. This configuration of New Grass Revival endured until they disbanded at the end of that decade, when each continued in individual endeavors.

The West Coast served as another focal point for the changing face of bluegrass. With its entertainment opportunities in television and film, as well as its status as a folk music mecca in the sixties, California was a natural breeding ground for opportunities in bluegrass, its bends and its blends. The "California sound" of new acoustic music in bluegrass came to be associated with fresh interpretations and unusual genre blending.

Two groups who found themselves in the right place at the right time were the Dillards, from Missouri, and the Kentucky Colonels, featuring Clarence and Roland White, originally from Maine. While the Kentucky Colonels appeared in a couple of early episodes, it was the Dillards who eventually became the core of the "Darling Family" on *The Andy Griffith Show*. They were real musicians playing real bluegrass, while "Sheriff Andy Taylor" often would pick and sing along with them. It was back porch bluegrass at its best on prime-time television.

Both groups attracted the attention of the college-tinged folk scene, gaining faithful followings. Clarence went on to become, for a time, a member of folk-rock's The Byrds, while Roland served stints with Bill Monroe, Lester Flatt, Country Gazette, Nashville Bluegrass Band, and now heads his own Roland White Band. Clarence, who joined forces with Peter Rowan, Bill Keith, David Grisman, and Richard Greene in Muleskinner, an essentially one-shot bluegrass supergroup, died tragically in 1973 when struck by a car.

The Dillards' repertoire leaned smartly on the folk book, adapting songs for bluegrass renditions. Setting them apart from most other bluegrass bands was their wonderful humor primarily fueled by bassist Mitch Jayne, whose keen wit and sense of comedic timing are legendary. In the seventies, they expanded to include more original material, with an electric-acoustic, country-bluegrass-rock sound. In recent years, they returned to the acoustic side of bluegrass.

Among the first bluegrass bands to feature the singing and songwriting of women, the Good Ol' Persons emerged in the Bay area in 1975. Several prominent women musicians passed through this influential group that maintained its Monroe-inspired edge without the inclusion of banjo in its earliest days, in itself an innovative move. Among others, Kathy Kallick is one of today's brightest songwriters and has one of the most expressively subtle voices, leading her own eponymous band. Fiddler-songwriter Laurie Lewis has since headed up a number of projects and performs frequently as a duo with mandolinist Tom Rozum. Her poised performances have a warm, spirited quality that sets Lewis apart. Many have recorded her memorable original songs.

Interestingly enough, a cornerstone of California bluegrass is not a "bend or blend" band but rather a group steeped in the classics of Monroe, the Stanleys, and Flatt and Scruggs. San Francisco's High Country has entertained audiences since 1968, offering high-energy traditional material as well as original songs written in the tradition.

Virginia-born, California-raised Tony Rice made his way back to the West Coast from Kentucky in the mid-seventies. In the Bluegrass State, he had been a member of the groundbreaking J.D. Crowe and the New South, whose use of drums and electric instruments marked that band as one of the most progressive for its time. The New South also sported, among others, two up-and-coming superpickers, multi-instrumentalist Ricky Skaggs and Jerry Douglas, who went on to give the dobro worldwide recognition. Back in California, Rice became a member of the David Grisman Quintet, whose new acoustic "Dawg" music gave priority to mandolin over banjo, exploring bluegrass in context with jazz and classical.

Inspired by Clarence White, Rice took flatpicking to new heights. His remarkably fluid, masterful style can be experienced today in the Tony Rice Unit. Older recordings that feature his extraordinary and instantly recognizable voice are treasures; in the 1990s, he lost it to muscle tension dysphonia. Nevertheless, according to at least one published interview, he does not miss it as much, perhaps, as his fans do and seems to view it more as an opportunity to explore further his guitar work.[2]

David Grisman has probably done as much for mandolin as Béla Fleck has for banjo, bringing it to new arenas, exploring music from bluegrass to Brazil. Originally active in the Greenwich Village folk music scene, Grisman had a longtime friendship with Grateful Dead anchor Jerry Garcia. Garcia played banjo and joined with Grisman, Peter Rowan, Dead bassist John Kahn, and "hillbilly jazz" fiddler Vassar Clements for some memorable bluegrass making in a short-lived (nine months in 1973) group, Old and In the Way.

A different "California sound" was introduced in the seventies by the exceptional trio of fiddler Byron Berline, flatpicking guitar stylist Dan Crary, and banjo picker John Hickman. The group's formidable range of instrumental virtuosity merged with a versatile repertoire that colorfully patchworked folk, jazz, classical, and country with bluegrass. Later, two additional musicians were added to the mix and the group became, aptly, "California." The band took a hiatus of several years but in 2003 returned to the road and recording studio.

WHAT GOES AROUND, STAYS AROUND

To continue this overview of the evolution of bluegrass, let me take you back in time to find out how one of today's top groups actually got its start nearly forty years ago.

It never ceases to amaze me that a music whose core sound has not changed largely in nearly six decades can still be so exciting, refreshing, and powerful in its presentation. The Del McCoury Band has won award after award in recent years, touching thousands around the world with its high-powered concerts and recordings. Legions of new and old fans flocked to hear them when they were part of a special concert tour package in celebration of the *O Brother, Where Art Thou?* music after it garnered its room's worth of industry honors. Here is an example of a group whose leader's "training years" were those within the tradition-based climate of the 1950s.

The Del McCoury Band performs in classic, traditional style; its repertoire embraces bluegrass standards but also incorporates contemporary pieces. Regardless, Del's bluesy tenor vocals, as intense as they are razor-edge sharp, are the epitome of the high lonesome sound that characterizes bluegrass.

His technique derives directly from the first generation of bluegrass artists. Del formed his first band in 1958 and moved on to work with the "master," Bill Monroe, from 1963 to 1964. He had been playing banjo

---

[2]Caroline Wright, "A Day in the Life of the World's Best Guitarist," *Listener* (July–August 2002): pp. 32–44.

primarily but was hired as guitarist and lead singer for the Blue Grass Boys. Monroe had hired someone else to fill the banjo slot, precocious Bill "Brad" Keith.

In 1967, Del put together his next group, the Dixie Pals, and in May 1981, the first of his two sons, fourteen-year-old Ronnie, joined him part-time playing mandolin. Son Robbie McCoury stepped up to the plate on banjo in 1987, and soon the name was changed to the Del McCoury Band. It was not long before the Del McCoury Band began to rack up music awards. The band has never shied from taking bluegrass to audiences outside its realm, collaborating with such artists as country's Steve Earle and alternative rock group Phish. In 2003, Del was inducted into the *Grand Ole Opry*, a pinnacle of achievement where bluegrass or country music is concerned.

Among countless others who have carried on traditional bluegrass, bandleaders Bill Harrell, Larry Sparks, and Doyle Lawson have injected special personal qualities into their music. Harrell paid his dues singing and playing mandolin and guitar in the 1950s in suburban D.C. and Maryland. With a warm, endearing voice, he spent a decade collaborating with banjo great Don Reno and the Tennessee Cut-Ups. In 1977, he re-formed one of his earlier groups, the Virginians, taking along with him bass-playing fellow Tennessee Cut-Up Ed Ferris, who remained with him for the next ten years. Harrell and band recorded numerous albums filled with bluegrass and country standards and originals. Harrell's expressive voice and the versatility of his talented sidemen always matched each other superbly.

Larry Sparks's musical resume is rather unusual in that he started at the top, beginning his professional career while in his teens in the 1960s working with the Stanley Brothers and then with Ralph Stanley's band. Sparks went on to found the Lonesome Ramblers in 1969, recording and touring ever since. His is one of the most unique voices, dubbed "the most soulful voice in bluegrass." His hot solos on guitar and "lonesome" instrumentals continue to set him apart.

From a gospel-singing Tennessee family, Doyle Lawson has been a bedrock of bluegrass gospel since forming Doyle Lawson and Quicksilver in 1979. The exquisitely honed hallmark of the group is its captivating quartet harmony singing. Not yet out of his teens, Lawson got a job playing banjo with Jimmy Martin. Switching from guitar, he moved on to sing tenor and play mandolin with revolutionary banjo player J.D. Crowe from 1966 to 1971, except for a six-month return engagement with Martin. From 1971 to 1979, he was a member of the progressive Country Gentlemen.

Of special note was the duo leadership of guitarist Bob Paisley and banjo stylist Ted Lundy. For roughly fifteen years, beginning in the early to mid-sixties, Lundy, Paisley, and the Southern Mountain Boys brought heartfelt bluegrass to fans. Lundy's was a musical family deeply entrenched in the traditional music of his Virginia Blue Ridge Mountains' home; among others, he had played with Ola Belle Reed's New River Boys. Following Lundy's death in 1980, Paisley regrouped as Bob Paisley and Southern Grass, which features his and Lundy's sons, and maintains the hard-driving traditional style backed by outstanding musicianship.

The Johnson Mountain Boys were an exceptional group, leaders of what has been called the "neo-traditionalist" movement. Founded in 1978, they were, without a doubt, the next decade's most popular traditional bluegrass ensemble. Wearing smartly styled suits and white cowboy hats, they gave precision-perfect, high-powered stage presentations that demonstrated instrumental prowess that could not get any better. The band captured the essence of the music in every detail.

During their ten-year tenure, a handful of personnel shifts took place. The sound remained characterized by cofounder Dudley Connell's crisp tenor vocals that nailed the high lonesome sound and quartet singing that left shivers running down the spine. However, circumstances precipitated a decision by the Johnson Mountain Boys to disband at the height of the group's popularity.

A farewell live recording was put to press and eventually nominated for a Grammy award. Following that and until 1996, in addition to individual pursuits, the Johnson Mountain Boys reunited from time to time for special engagements only. Connell currently sings lead for the Seldom Scene, while fiddle player Eddie Stubbs is now one of the distinctive voices announcing for the *Grand Ole Opry*.

"JMB" bass player Marshall Wilborn went on to join his wife and multiple award-winning musician-songwriter Lynn Morris in her band. Morris is a shining example of a successful woman in a lead role. The Lynn Morris Band artfully lets tradition meet creativity in its repertoire and stage shows.

Other dynamic groups who carry on the traditional sound today include David Davis and the Warrior River Boys, Karl Shiflett and Big Country Show, and the James King Band, to name a few. An interesting note emphasizing how bluegrass maintains an unbroken circle: Cleo Davis, the first Blue Grass Boy with Bill Monroe, signing on as guitarist-vocalist in 1939, was an uncle to David Davis.

Since the 1980s, bluegrass has developed exponentially along all the lines discussed and more. Country and pop crossover became another strong audience source for bluegrass, especially during that decade and into the next. Among those who appealed to the country set were Ricky Skaggs and Alison Krauss.

Skaggs, who had been a member of Ralph Stanley's group as well as country star Emmylou Harris's Hot Band, among others, emerged a country artist in his own right, racking up a roomful of awards while never forgetting his traditional roots. He returned to bluegrass in the late 1990s, retaining the stage polish perfected as a commercial country star. With his powerhouse

Kentucky Thunder band, Skaggs continues to bring flawless, pure bluegrass to audiences of all persuasions. Putting to good advantage his celebrity on many fronts, Ricky Skaggs has served the bluegrass community well as one of its most vocal and visible ambassadors.

By her mid-teens, Alison Krauss had already been featured in *People*, had won a string of awards at fiddle contests, had secured a recording contract, and was selected to represent Western long bow fiddle (Texas style) playing on the celebrated Masters of the Folk Violin tours. With her bandmates in Union Station, Krauss has opened new doors for contemporary bluegrass, introducing a lighter, pop-tinged side of the music to a younger audience as well as to country enthusiasts. The group keeps its legions of devoted bluegrass fans satisfied with great down-home picking. The range has been wide, but they have always remained rooted in bluegrass.

In 1993, at age twenty-one, Krauss was one of the youngest members ever to be invited to join the *Grand Ole Opry*. Furthermore, it was the first time in nearly thirty years a bluegrass act had been added to the *Opry* lineup. Alison Krauss + Union Station played key roles in the music of *O Brother, Where Art Thou?* and its companion documentary *Down from the Mountain*. Union Station member Dan Tyminski is the award-winning voice behind George Clooney's, as a member of the "Soggy Bottom Boys" singing "I Am a Man of Constant Sorrow." Krauss was also featured on the 2003 T Bone Burnett film soundtrack, *Cold Mountain*.

The popularity of IIIrd Tyme Out is almost cultlike. With Russell Moore at the helm, the band renders compelling harmonies. A polished stage presentation and superb musicianship have combined to contribute to the band's longevity and repeat award taking. In the same league is the Lonesome River Band whose numerous awards speak volumes about their talent and appeal. Many outstanding players have passed through the group's ranks since it first emerged in the late eighties.

With a contemporary flair and a fountainhead of talent, Rhonda Vincent and the Rage are among today's top bluegrass artists. Born in 1962, Vincent has been center-stage picking and singing since the age of three, starting out in her family's band, the Sally Mountain Show. In 1985, she switched gears to work in mainstream country only to return "home" to bluegrass. As seasoned as an entertainer can get, Vincent is a self-assured multi-instrumentalist with dynamic vocals; her side crew are some of the best in the business. As if one needed further proof that talent runs in the family, brother Darrin is a member of Ricky Skaggs's Kentucky Thunder.

A BLUEGRASS MELTING POT

The potpourri of urban cultural hotbeds has nurtured an intriguing diversity of genre mergers as far back as the seventies. In addition to the jazz-inflected bluegrass of Grisman and Trischka, mentioned earlier, three musicians stand out from the pack for their extensive accomplishments in bluegrass-derived music.

Life magazine named dobro player Jerry Douglas one of the ten best country musicians of all time. Deeply rooted in bluegrass, Douglas knows no boundaries when it comes to his imaginative compositions. In addition to the plethora of projects with which he is involved, he tours regularly with Alison Krauss + Union Station, as well as with The Whites—Buck, Sharon, and Cheryl, featured in *O Brother* and *Down from the Mountain*, and with whom Douglas first played from 1979 through 1985.

Internationally recognized, Douglas has taken dobro where no musician has ventured before and likely no other will ever be able to follow. One of the most sought-after studio musicians, he has embraced in his endeavors everything from country and Celtic to opera and jazz. He refers to his distinctive signature style as "that slidey sound." In the late eighties, he teamed with four other extraordinary musical minds to tour and record as Strength in Numbers. The quintet featured Douglas, Sam Bush, Béla Fleck, bassist-composer Edgar Meyer, and multi-instrumentalist Mark O'Connor, best known to worldwide audiences in his fiddler-violinist role.

Béla Fleck, mentioned earlier with New Grass Revival, was at one time a student under the tutelage of Tony Trischka. In 1989, he formed the Flecktones, a category-defying ensemble that tackles a mixed bag of acoustic and electronic bluegrass, jazz, world music, and funk. Fleck's talents, although bluegrass-initiated, place him on a plane of his own; like Douglas, he, too, has an open door policy on the music he invents.

Mark O'Connor has gone from winning fiddle championships at age twelve to being recognized as a world-class composer-musician in classical circles. Most often heard on fiddle, or violin, depending on the circumstances, O'Connor is well versed on guitar and mandolin as well and in his youth pursued banjo for a time. With powerfully driven bluegrass and Texas-style fiddling his inspiration, O'Connor has soared well beyond those confines. Comparisons to Dvořák come to mind, as do Copland's Americana-fueled works. O'Connor blends traditional Appalachian melodies with sophisticated classical and expressive jazz to create majestic pieces.

In the late seventies, Kentucky's McLain Family Band pioneered bringing bluegrass into the classical arena and on to the orchestral stage. A handful of others have done so since, although O'Connor's contributions are clearly the most comprehensive. In addition, some have included classical pieces in novel arrangements within eclectic bluegrass repertories. Among them are Dan Crary, Nitty Gritty Dirt Band's John McEuen, and Spontaneous Combustion from the greater Kansas City area.

On its Web page, Psychograss describes itself as "an instrumental bluegrass-based supergroup in the tradition of the great improvising modern jazz groups." The quintet goes well beyond the borders of jazz-grass to incorporate a multitude of influences that includes bluegrass, jazz, classical, and South American music.

Men do not have a corner on the jazz-grass market; Alison Brown, who toured for several years with Alison Krauss + Union Station, is a cut above, not only for her exceptional musicianship but also for her savvy as a music business professional. She continues to explore sophisticated jazz-hued music via banjo while keeping a hand in straight-ahead bluegrass.

New York City is America's original melting pot. Breakfast Special grew out of New York's Country Cooking in the seventies. It embraced the amalgam of ethnic influences found in New York City. Among others, it included fiddler Kenny Kosek and Cooking mandolinist Andy Statman. Incorporating traditional Jewish melodies and other ethnic infusions, the group explored the multicultural neighborhoods of the Big Apple in bluegrass context, adding a heavy dose of original material.

It is often difficult to separate Celtic fiddle tunes from bluegrass. With the roots of bluegrass originating in the spirited melodies and thoughtful ballads from across the pond, there is a natural blend. A sizeable number of nonbluegrass bands are "eclectic acoustic," offering a broad range of Celtic, folk, and bluegrass, and by doing so, demonstrate the close proximity each has to the other.

In addition, collaborations between Celtic and bluegrass artists have come into vogue. In recent years, the world-famous Chieftains, on their *Down the Old Plank Road* volumes, cross the Atlantic to join bluegrass performers Earl Scruggs, Ricky Skaggs, Del McCoury, and Alison Krauss, to name a few, in such traditional standards as "Sally Goodin" and "Give the Fiddler a Dram."

While the Celtic connection is an obvious marriage, that of klezmer with bluegrass might not be. Referred to informally as "Jewish jazz," klezmer music originated as Eastern European devotional and celebratory music of the Hasidic Jews, a religious sect that emphasizes mysticism, prayer, and joy. Enjoying its own renaissance much like bluegrass of late, modern klezmer contains elements ranging from lively, spirited dance tunes to soulfully introspective songs. Its similarities to bluegrass are striking: compare it with foot-stomping fiddle tunes and the bluesy, high lonesome songs of the American genre. Bluegrass, Celtic, and klezmer all thrive on the infinite improvisational possibilities in the hands of virtuoso musicians.

Andy Statman is today considered a master keeper of the klezmer flame. Not only a sensitive, well-versed bluegrass mandolin player, he is an extraordinary clarinetist who has probed the depth and breadth of klezmer music with renewed spirituality. He continues to bridge the two audiences, testament to both Statman's versatile abilities as well as to the natural connection between bluegrass and klezmer.

In the tradition and footsteps of Statman come Margot Leverett and the Klezmer Mountain Boys. Clarinetist Leverett, a founding member of the internationally acclaimed Klezmatics, is teamed with an exceptional ensemble, expert among them in bluegrass, klezmer, jazz, swing, classical, Broadway, rock, Irish, and country music. Among the "Boys" are ex-Skyline mandolinist Barry Mitterhoff and Breakfast Special's Kenny Kosek.

There are any number of additional klezmer-bluegrass collaborations floating around. The Fabrangen Fiddlers began playing bluegrass arrangements of Jewish melodies while parking lot picking at festivals. Today, they perform traditional and original Jewish music reflecting Middle Eastern, jazz, and bluegrass influences. The Diaspora Yeshiva Band is yet another that has tackled klezmer à la bluegrass.

Nickel Creek's three young core musicians, mandolin whiz kid Chris Thile and siblings Sara and Sean Watkins, fiddle and guitar, respectively, all honed their chops playing bluegrass. They have taken that training ground and have applied the precision of bluegrass technique to a whole other spectrum of music. With little, if any, resemblance to bluegrass, traditional or progressive, their original music connects the technical proficiency required in bluegrass with youthful, alternative acoustic blends of Beatles-flavored psychedelia, folk, pop, left-of-center rock, and other imaginative sounds. Oh, yes, did I mention that *Time* magazine named Nickel Creek as one of its musical innovators for the new millennium?

5

Fiddling to Flatpicking

Instrumental virtuosity is often an understatement in bluegrass; it is akin to high art. When watching or listening to the profusion of phenomenal players, one might be quick to believe they are from another planet. How do their fingers stay attached when flying across those strings? How do they get the equivalent of three marching bands' worth of notes out of one instrument? Certainly those hot licks weren't learned in elementary or even high school music classes.

Listening to and watching bluegrass being executed brings to mind words such as *riveting* and *enthralling*; it can leave you dumbstruck. And while first-generation musicians were no slouchers, today's bluegrass musicians are setting new standards, striving higher than ever before to find new notes on the scale and novel ways to let them loose.

To discover bluegrass, one has to remember that the "sound" is everything. Undeniably, song lyrics are vital, but without the instruments as backdrop to the words, there just would not be bluegrass. Well, okay, with the exception of spine-tingling quartet gospel singing *sans* instrumentation.

Fiddle tunes, for example, are one of the backbones of bluegrass, whether portrayed on fiddle, banjo, mandolin, or dobro. Strip down the music to some of the old duets of just fiddle and banjo talking to each other and you will hear the quiet but invigorating soul of the music. Just as in any music, you cannot close the dictionary and understand fully what bluegrass is until you have listened to it.

Ensemble interaction is the essence of bluegrass, but it takes individual instruments and players to make a group. Discussed in preceding chapters are the parallels bluegrass runs to jazz. Key to that is improvisation. Take a basic melody and expand from there. It could be with classic hot bluegrass licks or airy jazzlike explorations. One by one, group members will take a cue, almost magically, from each other, meeting or challenging the preceding soloist, until all meet at "home" at the song's end.

Energy is high while all this is happening. One musician's notes melt into the next instrument's down the line. As complex as a fully orchestrated symphony, virtuosic bluegrass musicians make it look easy, but they never play easy. Known for giving their all, bluegrass artists put more than fingers and arms into the mix; every number is delivered with gusto.

Regional styles within bluegrass have developed over the years that reflect fluctuations in repertoire or in delivery. Just as there were geographic centers as bluegrass developed along more progressive and blended lines, so too there are local or regional nuances in execution. Fiddle tunes, for example, often have many adaptations as well as names for the same tune, just as ballad songs have differed in lyrics from place to place, often taking a cue from local lore.

Among the numerous states or regions that nurture their own traditions are the Ozark Mountains, the Pinelands of southern New Jersey, as well as Texas and its surrounds. New Jersey's "Piney" music relies heavily on its own repertoire, for example, entrenched in the traditions of the people who have lived and worked there since it was first settled. The sound, however, is also distinctive, something of a cross between traditional bluegrass and classic early country.

Ozark-style fiddling represents some of the heartiest around and is highly reminiscent, in a raw-edged form, of the original Celtic lands from which the repertoire came. Prevalent mainly in Missouri and Arkansas, it can be as fierce as it can be sweet.

Texas-style fiddling, also known as Western long bow, was popularized primarily by Benny Thomasson. It involves an extended sweep of the arm, allowing more notes to emphasize with greater expression and drive a particular point in a tune. Mark O'Connor was directly influenced by and learned from Thomasson. Texas fiddling, although not the only, is one of the most popular competition styles in the many fiddle contests held around the country.

Of course, these differences do not confine themselves to fiddle but spill over to the ensemble sound. As you become more familiar with bluegrass, you will begin to distinguish not only these fluctuations but also their connections as you move from one artist to the next.

As it would take an encyclopedia to discuss, or even list, all the incredible players of bluegrass, I have provided information about only a select few influential figures. I have not repeated information here about those players discussed elsewhere in the book. Each section is supplemented by a short list of additional musicians, living and deceased, to check out. Because most have been members of more than one group, and, as explained earlier, personnel often shifts regularly, an Internet search is your fastest route to the most current information on a particular individual.

MANDOLIN

Bill Monroe spoke to the heart through his mandolin. He took the instrument out of parlors, classical orchestras, and European ethnic folk gatherings and provided a new home. Single-handedly, he gave it a voice that branded it "American." He leaned on and learned from many influences, including guitarists and fiddle players, blues and jazz genres, and dance rhythms.

Mandolin was taken to new heights by "Big Mon" as a lead instrument. The sweetness and power of this exquisite, elegant instrument was fully awakened in his hands. The "Father of Bluegrass" coaxed not just music out of his mandolin but an art form.

Italian mandolins originally were pear shaped and bowl backed. The classic "bluegrass" mandolin has a design and sound, developed in the early part of the twentieth century by the Gibson Company, that incorporates the upsweep scroll of a violin body and a flat back. The one used by Bill Monroe, and which remains the most popular style used in bluegrass, is the "F-5" model. "A" styles are also often found and more closely resemble the Italian mandolin. Tonal differences can be discerned.

Although Monroe was the original "mandolin master," others have been influential as the music has developed. Fast, clean, and unflappable could all describe the mandolin playing of Red Rector, who for several years was one of Carl Story's Rambling Mountaineers. Considered a bridge between first- and second-generation bluegrass musicians, Rector became more familiar to those who enjoyed his dynamic picking during the seventies and eighties while partnering with Bill Clifton on tours and recordings. He teamed up with jazz mandolinist Jethro Burns to record the album *Old Friends*, which, indeed, they were.

Jesse McReynolds created a mandolin technique called cross-picking. In simplistic terms, it involves picking the strings on both the up and down strokes to create rapid variations of repeated melodic patterns. McReynolds can take you seamlessly from a rapid-fire bluegrass tune to the snowy images portrayed in the film *Dr. Zhivago* with his beautiful rendition of "Somewhere My Love" ("Lara's Theme"). From there, he can kick you back to reality with rockin' chops on "Johnny B. Goode." McReynolds remains one of the most versatile mandolin players.

Roland White has had a mandolin in his hands since he was eight years old. However, it was another eight years before he first heard Bill Monroe and discovered bluegrass. That was in 1954, and White has been playing ever since, from the Country Boys, later called the Kentucky Colonels, to his current Roland White Band. His technique is confident and spirited, and his instructional approach is among the most respected.

Setting a standard that broke down barriers between bluegrass and rock-and-roll, Sam Bush is the original bluegrass rebel. Challenging the capabilities of both mandolin and fiddle since founding New Grass Revival in the seventies, he just as handily puts to the test bluegrass versus classical as he has done in his work with fellow mandolinist-fiddler Mike Marshall, composer and eclectic acoustic bassist Edgar Meyer, and world-renowned classical violinist Joshua Bell.

Mike Compton seems to play with the spirit of Bill Monroe deep within. His control and comprehension of mandolin are exceptional. His quietly inspired picking can be heard with such artists as the Nashville Bluegrass Band and John Hartford, including his participation in the *O Brother* projects as a "Soggy Bottom Boy."

Additional mandolin players to check out: Butch Baldassari, Wayne Benson, Jesse Brock, Jimmy Gaudreau, Doyle Lawson, Ronnie McCoury, David McLaughlin, Jeff Midkiff, Barry Mitterhoff, Bobby Osborne, John Reischman, Don Rigsby, Ricky Skaggs, Orrin Star, Adam Steffey, Frank Wakefield, Buck White, Josh Williams, Radim Zenkl.

BANJO

Time and again you will hear a bluegrass banjo player cite learning from folk music legend Pete Seeger's book, *How to Play the 5-String Banjo*. Originally published in 1948, the book underwent revision in 1954 to address the then new three-finger style picking evolving in bluegrass. For years, this was the bible, the only instructional book available for banjo pickers looking to grasp Scruggs-style picking. Eric Weissberg, who "delivered" "Dueling Banjos" in *Deliverance*, studied banjo with Seeger.

Popular exposure to banjo has come from, among others, an unexpected source, well-known actor Steve Martin. In his early career in the 1970s as a stand-up comic and during *Saturday Night Live* stints, he would play bluegrass banjo occasionally as part of his act. In reality, Martin is a serious player, who, along with high school pal John McEuen (Nitty Gritty Dirt Band), learned at the knee of Doug Dillard (The Dillards). In recent years, he has been spotted on talk shows, banjo in hand, delighting studio audiences on such network talk programs as ABC's *Live with Regis and Kelly* and NBC's *Ellen*. His last comedy album, *The Steve Martin Brothers*, included several of his instrumental originals. In 1999, Martin authored a splendid article in which he details his discovery of bluegrass and banjo.[1]

Over and above the many seminal players touched on in earlier chapters, Eddie Adcock stands out for his contribution. As far back as when he was a Blue Grass Boy and then as a member of the groundbreaking "classic" Country Gentlemen, Adcock pushed the envelope, kicking off the second-generation, newgrass approach to banjo. In fact, he boldly proclaimed as

[1]Marc Smirnoff, ed., *Best of the Oxford American: Ten Years from the Southern Magazine of Good Writing* (Athens, GA: Hill Street Press, 2002), p. 279.

much (and rightfully so) when he formed II Generation in the early 1970s. The sound was fresh, with intricate arrangements that reflected Adcock's interests outside of bluegrass in rock and folk. Also a sensitive fingerstyle guitarist, he draws from Merle Travis's guitar playing to execute his innovatively sculpted banjo technique. He continues to expand musical horizons with his wife, Martha, a top-notch rhythm guitar player-vocalist-songwriter. Days away from his sixty-fifth birthday, when I chatted with Eddie at the Wind Gap (Pennsylvania) Bluegrass Festival in June 2003, he quipped about bluegrass musicians and their longevity performing the music: "We love to do what we do."

Alan Munde has an exquisitely relaxed grace in his banjo playing. After time "served" with Jimmy Martin and the Sunny Mountain Boys, he anchored Country Gazette for twenty-one years. Munde is a leading banjo instructor and since 1986 has been affiliated with the bluegrass and country music program at South Plains College in west Texas, in addition to performing with his Alan Munde Gazette.

Butch Robins is extraordinary. His credits are many and varied, from playing for a brief period in New Grass Revival to establishing The Bluegrass Band, a short-lived forerunner of the Nashville Bluegrass Band (of which he is not a member), to working with "Mr. Monroe." His first solo recording, *Forty Years Late*, referred to Robins's feeling that he should have been born in an earlier era, that of bluegrass music's formative years. One could just as accurately describe his innovative, complex compositions as "forty years too soon"; he was ahead of the times long before anyone recognized it.

Part of a younger generation of "fast and clean" pickers, Sammy Shelor demonstrates technical proficiency par excellence. He plays in a confident, spirited manner and inspires by example. Since 1990, he has held the banjo post for the award-winning Lonesome River Band, whose emphasis is on traditional bluegrass with a rock-and-roll edge.

While clawhammer (frailing) banjo is generally a component of old-time music, any number of bluegrass artists have incorporated it into their repertoires. Among them have been Becky Buller, Raymond W. McLain, Lynn Morris, Vicki Simmons, Doc Watson, Merle Watson, and Linda Williams.

Additional banjo players to check out: Tom Adams, Jimmy Arnold, Terry Baucom, Kristin Scott Benson, Bob Black, Marty Cutler, Bill Emerson, Raymond Fairchild, John Hartford, Courtney Johnson, Jens Krüger, Steve Lutke, Larry McNeely, Jim Mills, Sonny Osborne, Allen Shelton, Bobby Thompson, Scott Vestal.

FIDDLE

While Scruggs-style banjo sealed the bluegrass sound, fiddle certainly infused it with drive as well as soul. It has been called the "devil's instrument" or the "devil's box" for the frenzy it can work up, and, therefore, thought by puritan observers to be a sinful undertaking. Arguably, the fiddle is the most versatile of bluegrass instruments, with a hefty range of practitioners whose interpretations are just as diversified.

As described in chapter 2, fiddle was a lively and integral aspect of Colonial life. In fact, fiddle competitions date at least to the 1730s. Today, there are numerous fiddlers' "conventions" and championships held around the country addressing a wide variety of styles. A sampling includes the oldest, continuous one, Fiddler's Grove Ole Time Fiddler's & Bluegrass Festival® in Union Grove, North Carolina, founded in 1924; the Old Fiddler's Convention, established in 1935 in Galax, Virginia; the National Oldtime Fiddlers' Contest® and Festival in Weiser, Idaho, begun in 1953; and the Smithville (Tennessee) Fiddlers' Jamboree, started in 1972.

Breakdowns and waltzes are two well-known types of fiddle tunes. Breakneck speed prevails on breakdowns, as the name implies, and three-quarter-beat waltz time is found in most every context of music. Irish reels, hornpipes, and jigs all show up in bluegrass repertoires.

Kenny Baker is considered *the* bluegrass fiddler. He spent a total of more than two decades playing alongside Bill Monroe. His father and grandfather were traditional fiddlers, but Baker's first instrument was the guitar. While in the Navy playing in a band at the USO, by default, he was designated "fiddler" when they were lacking one for dances. After being discharged, he maintained his musical interests, but they did not particularly lie with bluegrass. Although he enjoyed the traditional old tunes, it was the Western swing of Bob Wills and the "hot" swing jazz of Stephane Grappelli that really awoke Baker's sensibilities.

Circumstances took Baker out of the coal mines and into music when he was hired as a country fiddler for Don Gibson. Baker's talent eventually caught the ear of Monroe, and he was asked to join the Blue Grass Boys, where his fiddling style was shaped by what Monroe demanded for his bluegrass sound. His tone, attack, and smooth bowing all distinguish the technique he developed and perfected working with "Big Mon." His love of Western and jazz swing, along with the sound initially guided by Monroe, all contributed to Baker's outstanding portrayal of bluegrass.

Kenny Baker's influence is heard in such excellent younger players as Blaine Sprouse and Glen Duncan. Sprouse, who has often served as a complementary twin-fiddle match for Baker on recordings, has worked with such groups as Jim and Jesse and the Virginia Boys and the Osborne Brothers. Duncan has followed a similar path, also having worked with Jim and Jesse and the Osbornes, as well as with Bill Monroe and others. He currently tours with Earl Scruggs.

Two-time National Fiddle Champion at Weiser, Byron Berline brought Texas-style influence to Bill Monroe and His Blue Grass Boys, if only for his short time as a member in the sixties. His competitive edge and expertise in the style infused the now classic recording with Monroe of the traditional

"Sally Goodin'." His distinctive fiddling has filled out Country Gazette as well as Berline-Crary-Hickman, and then California.

Curly Ray Cline and Mack Magaha were both known for their fiery stage presence, as well as injecting more of the old-time sound into their playing. Both would back up their fiddling with modified dancing or dancelike movements. Cline, an original member of his family-based Lonesome Pine Fiddlers, played in Ralph Stanley's band for nearly thirty years, while Magaha was with Don Reno and Red Smiley between 1955 and 1964, then moved on to work primarily in country music.

Benny Martin, best known for his tenure spent fiddling with Flatt and Scruggs, was a passionate fiddler who projected an enhanced sense of dynamics and phrasing in his playing. The very full tone he coaxed from his instrument gave the impression of multiple fiddles. John Hartford described Martin's playing as doing so "with his whole body." Martin's wholehearted technique and all-encompassing sound grabbed Hartford by the shirt collar as a teenager and affected the course his life would take.

John Hartford was an extraordinary, if not unique, entertainer. One who could not be easily categorized because so much of what he did was wholly original, Hartford created his own niche simply by virtue of his many talents. He loved bluegrass and he loved fiddle tunes, just as he loved steamboatin'. He was a licensed riverboat pilot. These were his passions.

He could fill a band playing solo. A talented multi-instrumentalist, a gifted songwriter, and a natural storyteller, Hartford is best known as the composer of "Gentle on My Mind," a hit in the 1960s for country-pop singer Glen Campbell on whose weekly television variety show he often appeared. But to fans in bluegrass and folk circles, Hartford was a bridge to the world of traditional music.

In the final years before his death in 2001, Hartford pursued and promoted the fiddle music of Ed Haley. Born in 1883 in West Virginia and blind since age three, Haley was an unusual and influential fiddler whose playing and broad range of styles set him apart in the early part of the twentieth century.

Self-taught fiddler Bobby Hicks is a former Blue Grass Boy who played on Monroe's original recordings of such classic instrumentals as "Wheel Hoss," "Big Mon," and "Scotland." He worked with Ricky Skaggs for more than twenty years, both in Skaggs's country band as well as in Kentucky Thunder. Over the years, he has developed a broad range of expertise, complementing his perfected bluegrass fiddling with swing and other influences, which he continues to employ as fiddler with Jesse McReynolds and the Virginia Boys.

Two fiddlers who have injected a potpourri of genres into their bluegrass playing are Richard Greene and Vassar Clements. Greene's legacy has been disseminated via such trendsetting groups as the rock-fusion Seatrain, which also featured fellow renegade ex-Blue Grass Boy Peter Rowan, supergroup

Muleskinner also with Rowan, and his own The Grass Is Greener. Fiery fiddler Scotty Stoneman groomed Greene in his early days.

Legendary Vassar Clements is billed as the "Father of Hillbilly Jazz." For certain, his playing is so versatile that it stands above all the rest. At the age of fourteen while still in school, Clements had the opportunity to play with Bill Monroe; he became a regular Blue Grass Boy in 1949 and remained until 1956. He has gone on to work with a diverse roster that has included Jim and Jesse, Earl Scruggs, John Hartford, the Grateful Dead, Paul McCartney, the Allman Brothers, Northern Lights, and Stephane Grappelli. He appears on all three volumes of *Will the Circle Be Unbroken*.

Lighting fires among the younger set are Aubrey Haynie and Andy Leftwich. Entering his thirties in 2004, Haynie is a Mark O'Connor disciple and a much sought-after studio musician. Leftwich is even younger; born in 1981, his mastery of fiddle is precocious, as is his Celtic- and jazz-infused tune writing. He began his professional career at age fifteen with Valerie Smith and Liberty Pike. In 2001 Leftwich joined Ricky Skaggs and Kentucky Thunder.

Additional fiddlers to check out: Chris Brashear, Jimmy Buchanan, Luke Bulla, Becky Buller, Jason Carter, Michael Cleveland, Casey Driessen, Stuart Duncan, Howdy Forrester, Randy Howard, Kenny Kosek, Barbara Lamb, Laurie Lewis, Rickie Simpkins, Art Stamper, Ron Stewart, Eddie Stubbs, Jim Van Cleve, Johnny Warren, Paul Warren, Travis Wetzel.

GUITAR

Bluegrass guitar is almost as diversified in approaches as fiddle. Typically in bluegrass, flatpicking is employed, as opposed to fingerstyle, commonly utilized in acoustic blues, jazz, and classical forms. The strings are struck with a flat plectrum, or pick, held between the thumb and index fingers. As discussed in chapter 2, the development of flatpicking guitar playing goes back to Maybelle Carter. It is from her approach that modern flatpicking evolved. However, even among flatpickers, there are individual styles.

The leading proponent of the flatpicking technique and one of the most influential folk and country guitarists ever is Arthel "Doc" Watson. He is one of a handful of artists who emerged during the folk boom that came to be closely associated with bluegrass in spite of their not really fitting the mold. His earliest commercial exposure took place at such folk haunts as Gerdes' Folk City and the Gaslight in New York City's Greenwich Village.

While his music is often referred to as bluegrass, Watson is the first to tell you otherwise; his repertoire embraces mountain ballads to the Moody Blues. Many of the fiddle tunes he popularized with his flatpicking guitar method, however, are considered bluegrass standards today. The speed, precision, and beauty with which he plays can best be described as mesmerizing.

Born March 3, 1923, near what is now Deep Gap, North Carolina, Watson first learned Carter style when he picked up guitar at around age thirteen. He ascertained how to hold a pick from the way old-time jazz guitarist Nick Lucas held his. Beyond that, his influences ran wide, starting with the jazz and country guitar playing of fiddle tunes by Hank Garland and Grady Martin to the blues of Mississippi John Hurt, Furry Lewis, and the duo of Sonny Terry and Brownie McGhee, all the way to fifties' rockabilly.

In 1960, folklorist Ralph Rinzler discovered Doc Watson playing at a festival in his native North Carolina and eventually introduced him to the folk community at the 1963 Newport Folk Festival, where the blind guitarist was embraced enthusiastically. This appearance was followed by one in 1964 at New York City's Town Hall on a concert program with Bill Monroe. From that time forward, Doc's renown grew worldwide. His talent was passed on to his son, Merle, who performed with his father from the age of fifteen until his tragic death in a tractor accident in 1985. Merle, like his dad, was also a spirited clawhammer banjo player. Richard, Merle's son and Doc's grandson, often pairs with Doc on guitar, focusing on blues tunes.

Doc Watson's main picking partner since Merle's death has been Jack Lawrence. Lawrence is an outstanding flatpicker who more than rises to the occasion to meet the challenge of playing alongside such a larger-than-life legend as Doc. His speed and agility are flawless.

Watson reminisced a bit, chatting backstage at a concert in Englewood, New Jersey, November 7, 2002. As he has explained previously in interviews with me and with countless other journalists, Doc restated and emphasized how he views the music he plays:

> My interest in music started a way before bluegrass music, in the real sense, was born. I heard people on the radio, and on the old Victrola before the radio, that kind of started out hillbilly music, [as] we used to call it, the grass roots they call it now, or roots and branches. On WJJD [in Chicago], there was a "Suppertime Frolic," way back, and there was a duo on there, Mac and Bob.[2] One of the songs I remember that they sang, that Charlie and Bill [Monroe] grabbed and recorded, was "What Does the Deep Sea Say?" And that was my introduction to the hillbilly, or grassroots music.
>
> I've said this to many reporters, and you can use it to quote: "What do you call your music?" "I call it traditional, plus whatever else I want to play!" (*laughing*) That's a blunt answer, but it's true. I might want to do one of Hoagy Carmichael's tunes. . . . It doesn't have anything to do with bluegrass, but it's music. I never could stick in one niche. I'm a wanderer in music; I like a *lot* of it.

[2]Mac and Bob (a.k.a. Lester McFarland and Robert A. Gardner) first met and began singing together while both were students at the Kentucky School for the Blind in 1915. McFarland's mandolin playing is recognized as influential in popularizing the instrument among early country musicians, and some of their songs worked their way into the standard bluegrass repertoire.

Among those influenced by Doc Watson was the Kentucky Colonels' Clarence White. White took Doc's flatpicking technique and injected a rhythmic swing and unusual syncopation. Dan Crary, mentioned in the previous chapter, is another major influential and creative flatpicking stylist, as is Norman Blake. Crary's style reflects a sophisticated, contemporary bent.

Norman Blake is generally considered outside the bluegrass realm, yet his music is often found there. A multi-instrumentalist equally fluent on guitar, mandolin, fiddle, and dobro, his diverse musical credits include not only his solo work and that with wife, Nancy, but also with such artists as the Carter Family, Bill Monroe, Bob Dylan, Joan Baez, John Hartford, Johnny and June Carter Cash, Michelle Shocked, Kris Kristofferson, and Steve Earle. In addition, he was a participant on the original *Will the Circle Be Unbroken* recording. Blake is featured in the *O Brother, Where Art Thou?* project, singing Louisiana Governor Jimmie Davis's "You Are My Sunshine." It is through such affiliations and with his input of a more "old-timey" side of flatpicking that Blake, too, has advanced the style appreciably for bluegrass.

Innovation by younger players has given flatpicking guitar an entirely different language since the early 1990s. Such pickers as Beppe Gambetta from Italy, David Grier, and Bryan Sutton have taken the technique to new heights and speeds.

Equally important in the ensemble sound is rhythm guitar playing. Lester Flatt surely set the standard in this regard. Dependable, strong rhythm is critical to the drive in bluegrass. Many rhythm players are also equally adept at playing lead.

Additional guitarists to check out: Russ Barenberg, Audie Blaylock, John Carlini, Joe Carr, Bob Harris, Clay Hess, Jim Hurst, Chris Jones, Steve Kaufman, Cody Kilby, Del McCoury, Peter McLaughlin, Mark Newton, Scott Nygaard, Don Reno, Ronnie Reno, Charles Sawtelle, James Shelton, George Shuffler, Kenny Smith, Larry Sparks, Tim Stafford, Orrin Star, Dan Tyminski, Jeff White.

BASS

In the all-important backfield found in virtually every bluegrass ensemble is the bass player. Whether acoustic or electric, bass is designated timekeeper for the group. Who *sets* the time—bassist or a different musician—varies, but the bass player must maintain it for everyone to follow.

Bluegrass has witnessed many an outstanding bassist. Ed Ferris, sideman with such greats as Don Reno, Bill Harrell, and the Country Gentlemen, was exceptional not only for his exquisite playing but also for his endearing personality. In an interview with me in the mid-eighties, Ferris cited Jake Tullock, who worked with Lester Flatt and Earl Scruggs, as his primary influence.

Two bass playing Huskeys have left an indelible mark in bluegrass. Roy Huskey, Jr., known as "Junior" Huskey, was one of the greatest country session players to ever come through Nashville; he appeared along with John Hartford and Clarence White on the Byrds' crossover country roots project, *Sweetheart of the Rodeo*. He came to the attention of bluegrass primarily through his work on the seminal *Will the Circle Be Unbroken* recording.

His son, also Roy, was dubbed "Roy Jr." by admiring peers when Roy Jr. stepped into his professional career shortly after the death of his father in 1971 and right after the making of the *Circle* album. A classy, on-the-mark musician, Roy Jr. was as much if not more in demand for studio work in Nashville. Roy Jr. appeared on the second *Circle* CD, as well as on hundreds of bluegrass and country projects. He also toured with such artists as Emmylou Harris, Peter Rowan, the O'Kanes, Steve Earle, and T Bone Burnett, and had an especially close performing relationship with John Hartford. Sadly, both Huskeys were lost to cancer in the prime of their careers, the senior at age forty-three, the son at forty.

Jack Cooke has been an enduring figure in Ralph Stanley's Clinch Mountain Clan since 1970. In addition, he worked in the fifties with both Ralph and Carter Stanley. He did a stint with Bill Monroe and with the Stoneman Family as well. Cooke's playing is solid, intuitive, and a true hallmark of traditional bluegrass.

Clean, consistent, traditional bass playing is also heard in that of the Lynn Morris Band's Marshall Wilborn and Mark Hembree, who is a veteran of such groups as Buck White and the Down Home Folks, Bill Monroe and the Blue Grass Boys, and the Nashville Bluegrass Band. From the Del McCoury Band is neo-traditionalist bass player Mike Bub. Bub, a founding member of Weary Hearts, also previously worked with Bill Monroe and the Osborne Brothers. Some of his expert training derived from his bluegrass music studies at South Plains College in Levelland, Texas.

Two splendid examples of contemporary players with eclectic tastes are Missy Raines and T. Michael Coleman. Coleman, playing electric, was a long-time sideman with Doc and Merle Watson, later moving on to play bass with the Seldom Scene as well as with another group also involving the Scene's Mike Auldridge, Chesapeake.

Multiple award winner Missy Raines for many years toured and recorded with Eddie and Martha Adcock. Along with guitarist-vocalist Jim Hurst, Raines has created an unusual niche for bass as a lead instrument in bluegrass-based music filled with jazz innovation, something she refers to as "hybridized" music. She looks to Tom Gray, as well as to Todd Phillips and Rob Wasserman, as inspiration and influence. Phillips's extensive credits with other genre benders and blenders include David Grisman, J.D. Crowe, and Psychograss, while Wasserman has worked with Grisman, Jerry Garcia, Stephane Grappelli, and a host of other legendary jazz artists.

Mark Schatz is a multi-instrumentalist and dancer. Twice awarded honors for his exceptional bass playing, he also plays mandolin and clawhammer banjo. His clog dancing is equally well known from his work with the Footworks Percussive Dance Ensemble. Among the many he has performed with are John Hartford, David Grisman, Tim and Mollie O'Brien, Béla Fleck, Emmylou Harris, Jerry Douglas, Nickel Creek, as well as with his own hand-picked Mark Schatz and Friends.

Additional bass players to check out: Barry Bales, John Cowan, Dennis Crouch, Mark Fain, Laurie Lewis, Gene Libbea, Molly Mason, Ruth McLain, Vicki Simmons, Terry Smith, Jim Watson, Cheryl White.

DOBRO

The dobro is an acoustic resonator or resophonic stringed instrument. It is typically played in a horizontal position. The first guitar with a resonator was the National silver steel resonator guitar, invented in 1926 by John Dopyera, Sr., a partner in the National Company. Dopyera, Sr. left National and, with his brothers in 1928, formed the Dobro Company where the dobro was patented. The name "DOBRO" was chosen because it not only represented "DO-pyera BRO-thers," but also derives from the Slovak word for *good*. The Dopyera family had immigrated to California in 1908 from the Austro-Hungarian monarchy that became Czechoslovakia in 1919.

The impetus for creating such an instrument was to have a "guitar" that could hold its own in the pit orchestras of vaudeville, where guitars were typically drowned out by trombones and other bolder instruments. The challenge was how to amplify sound without distortion.

Hawaiian music was in its heyday of popularity in the twenties. With its breezy, swaying sound, it became the first market for the new steel guitar. These guitars had square necks and were played horizontally, lap style. In the very early thirties, a round-neck version became popular in cowboy movies but was played in the more familiar upright guitar-playing position. Steel-bodied National dobros became popular among blues musicians in the thirties who often could be found playing in the rain on the streets, trying to earn money; rain could not do to a steel guitar what it could to a traditional wood one. It also stood up well in bar fights, common in those days.

Today, virtually all "bluegrass" dobros are wood-bodied construction with an aluminum resonator, a bright chrome cover plate, "spider"-style bridge, raised nut, and square neck. At least three-dozen individual luthiers (makers of stringed instruments) and major musical instrument companies manufacture them worldwide.

From 1939 and for the next fifty-plus years, Bashful Brother Oswald (Beecher "Pete" Kirby) played dobro for the "King of Country Music," Roy Acuff and the Smoky Mountain Boys. While others had played it previously, he was the first dobro player to bring it front and center, giving it a major voice in the band. This opened the door for its later, more prominent role in bluegrass. Oswald is another of the legends that appears on the 1972 *Will the Circle Be Unbroken* recording.

It was Uncle Josh Graves (Burkett "Buck" Graves) who, while working with Lester Flatt and Earl Scruggs, gave the dobro its permanent relevance in bluegrass. Proficient on guitar and mandolin as well, Uncle Josh also worked with Wilma Lee and Stoney Cooper and, since the eighties, has teamed with fiddler Kenny Baker, displaying their virtuosic talents.

Around the same time that Jerry Douglas was beginning to make the rounds, a prolific musician from North Carolina was further establishing the dobro's place on the *Grand Ole Opry* stage. Gene Wooten performed there with Wilma Lee Cooper and the Clinch Mountain Clan and later with the Osborne Brothers. He had a debonair flair and a sensitive, compelling style. A popular studio musician, Wooten also worked with such artists as Patty Loveless, Country Gazette, and Nashville's Sidemen.

Arguably, the dobro's most ardent pioneering supporter, Tut Taylor, continues to champion the dobro in bluegrass; he has been playing, building, and praising them since the earliest bluegrass years. Taylor, also a fine mandolinist, adapted fiddle tunes for dobro utilizing an innovative style akin to cross-picking. He appears on a much sought after, untitled collector's item that brought together an array of amazing musicians: Norman Blake, Butch Robins, Sam Bush, Vassar Clements, country-jazz mandolinist Jethro Burns, and jazz bassist the legendary Dave Holland. In addition to these, he has toured, recorded, and jammed with a diverse roster that has included everyone from John Hartford to Clarence and Roland White to rock star Leon Russell.

A member of the original Seldom Scene, Mike Auldridge gave the dobro its first ultracontemporary voice, adding a sophisticated zest to the sound, influenced by the rock and folk-pop repertoire of the day. Also known for his pedal and lap steel playing, he has gone on to a number of projects since that time, including the eclectic acoustic Chesapeake, the trio Auldridge-Bennett-Gaudreau, and the Good Deale Bluegrass Band. Seldom Scene and Country Gentlemen cofounder John Duffey, primarily known as a mandolin player, also played dobro and can be heard doing so on early Country Gentlemen recordings.

Stacy Phillips is known as an accomplished fiddle player and dobro stylist. He stands out for his unique approach to tunes. A member in the seventies of New York City's multiculturally influenced Breakfast Special, Phillips continues to show a rainbow of colors in his deft playing.

From 1977 through 1996, a member of the Good Ol' Persons, Sally Van Meter is an exceptional and in-demand musician. She has collaborated with such performers as David Grisman, Jerry Garcia, Tony Rice, Chris Hillman, country music's Mary-Chapin Carpenter, Alison Brown, blues great Taj Mahal, bluegrass vocalist Claire Lynch, Irish artists Gerry O'Beirne and Maura O'Connell, and the inimitable Leftover Salmon. In addition, she has worked in film, radio, and television including CBS's *Northern Exposure*.

Additional dobro stylists to check out: Norman Blake, Curtis Burch, Cindy Cashdollar, Jimmy Heffernan, Dan Huckabee, Rob Ickes, Beverly King, Randy Kohrs, Phil Leadbetter, Kevin Maul, Fred Travers.

BLUEGRASS COUSINS

Among the instruments that preceded the "hard-core" bluegrass sound were the autoharp and the accordion. Autoharp, essentially a chorded zither, was invented in the late 1800s and gained popularity in the United States around the turn of the twentieth century. The pioneering country music Carter Family is probably the best known group that featured it, as did the Stoneman Family.

Autoharp saw a resurgence in popularity in the sixties and early seventies when the Carters came back into the public eye, partially as a result of the folk boom as well as their appearances with the Johnny Cash show. In addition, "Mother" Maybelle Carter played autoharp on the first *Will the Circle Be Unbroken* album. Folk-rock artist John Sebastian, lead singer of the Lovin' Spoonful, featured it prominently in that group's concerts and recordings during the sixties. Mike Seeger continues to perform with it as well as numerous other instruments, as he did with the New Lost City Ramblers.

In bluegrass, Bill Clifton has featured autoharp in much of his work. Multi-instrumentalist Little Roy Lewis often plays autoharp for a number or two during Lewis Family shows. Actually, Roy is known to play several different instruments in succession within any given song, switching from one to the next in the blink of an eye. During the last quarter century, Bryan Bowers has successfully performed as a solo artist with autoharp, masterfully picking out traditional fiddle tunes and ballads, straying into the bluegrass repertoire with borderline material.

Often overlooked, yet well-documented is Sally Ann Forrester's contribution of accordion to Bill Monroe's act for a number of years in the forties. She is featured on the 1945 Columbia recordings of Bill Monroe and the Blue Grass Boys. It should also be noted that it was not uncommon to use piano in the early days. Piano, or keyboards, continues to be used today in contra dance music, discussed in chapter 2.

In old-time mountain music, the Appalachian, or mountain, dulcimer was often the instrument of choice in lieu of guitar accompaniment to the solo voice. Jean Ritchie, discussed in the previous chapter, is one of the best known practitioners of this dulcimer. Variations of the Appalachian dulcimer are found in such countries as Norway (*langeleik*), Germany (*scheitholt*), Sweden (*humle*), and Iceland (*langspil*).

The instrument has a long sound box, similar to that of a violin body, and a fretboard over which three, sometimes four, strings pass. Usually played flat on the lap (hence, alternately called a lap dulcimer), the dulcimer is fretted with a "noter," often a thin stick of bamboo or similar item, and strummed or struck preferably with a feather quill or a guitar pick.

Looking outside the realm of bluegrass to the more eclectic acoustic bands, that is those that incorporate bluegrass but do not perform it exclusively, hammered dulcimer can sometimes be found lending its sweet tones to the mix. Walt Michael and Company is one such group known for adapting hammered dulcimer to the broad catalog of fiddle tunes found in bluegrass and in music from the Celtic Isles.

SUPERGROUPS AND BEYOND

Bluegrass has a long history of "supergroups," ensemble playing involving "star" pickers and singers. The idea possibly evolved from the long-standing tradition of closing an evening's performance or a festival weekend with an extended encore featuring all the program participants on stage, often in a grand jam, sometimes going on for a marathon length of time until virtually every picker has taken a solo break.

The first supergroup that comes to mind was the 1973 Muleskinner, mentioned earlier. Since that time, other "dream" bands that have either recorded together or have given limited performances are such groups as the Rounder (Records) Banjo Extravaganza, Longview, all-women Blue Rose, WhiteHouse, Strength in Numbers, and the precocious Chicks with Picks, a.k.a. Calamity Jane, whose lineup includes preteen multi-instrumentalist Sierra Hull.

A conversation took place in the fall of 2002 with a seventy-something newcomer to bluegrass. An open-minded music aficionado knowledgeable more in such areas as classical, Broadway, and ragtime, he had attended a "Down from the Mountain Tour" concert in which artists and music from *O Brother, Where Art Thou?* and the subsequent documentary were featured. Previously, he had never shown any special affinity to bluegrass, although I knew he had heard it. So I asked why he chose to attend this presentation.

His response was, "I thought there would be more of the same type of music I heard in *O Brother*; that's what I wanted. Before the concert, I had had a whole different impression of who Ricky Skaggs was. What an incredible musician!"

The gentlemen went on to inform me that he had purchased a Del McCoury CD, which rather surprised me coming from him. Therefore, I further inquired what it was he liked about the McCoury band's performance in particular.

"It was just so outstanding," he said ardently. "Every one of them was such an outstanding musician. It just floored me to see how beautifully they blended in an ensemble like that. And Del's voice, high pitched, seemed to be perfect for the vocals. I got very enthusiastic about the group."

These words sum up well the experience of hearing and seeing bluegrass live. This new fan of bluegrass was my own father. Believe me when I tell you that I was the one caught off guard by his attraction to bluegrass; I had no idea my own dad liked bluegrass...well, he didn't, not really, until he heard the music portrayed in the Coen Brothers' film. This, from a dad whose daughter had worked in bluegrass for more than a quarter century.

Who's hot and who's not tends to go through cycles in bluegrass, as in any musical genre, with a number of Beatles/Elvis-like mainstays. What always remains is the enduring sound and the recordings the "old-timers" leave to make way for the new kids on the block. Neither should be dismissed. The "old" guys are who the "young 'uns" learned from and continue to learn from.

New talent emerges each year, and the artists seem to keep improving on perfection, or at the very least, on excellence.

Musicianship is the cornerstone and the pinnacle of bluegrass music. But let's not forget the songs. Where would the high lonesome sound be if not for words to sing straight from the heart, right into the soul. . . . ?

6

Songs of Love, Death, Faith, and Family

Legendary songwriters Tom T. and Dixie Hall say, "It all begins with a song." Bluegrass songs, like much of country's, portray the very real, everyday lives of those singing them.

In its earliest years, a large portion of the bluegrass repertoire depended on the traditional ballads and hymns handed down for generations and given a new suit of clothes by the emerging genre. As bluegrass developed, so did a catalog that spoke to the emotions of the people playing it as well as those of their audience.

Love, death, faith, and family were central themes, and they endure in today's richly supplemented selection of original material. A different spark set the largely similar themes apart in their settings of the sixties and seventies, modernized for a younger generation.

There is likely not a genre in the world that does not rely on matters of the heart for the bulk of its material. Death is inevitable, also a universal theme, while yearning for the homeplace is key in the family-oriented songs of bluegrass.

Gospel songs continue to be strong portraits that provide a glimpse into the lives of many of the artists who were brought up surrounded by church traditions often rendered in song. From inspirational hymns to lively outpourings of praise and joy, numerous songs touch on the nerves of one's beliefs regardless of religious background. The emotion that bluegrass gospel songs evoke is tremendously moving.

An overview of bluegrass songs would not be complete without first mentioning those of Bill Monroe as well as those written *about* him and his music. His have become standards.

Love and love lost are themes that run deep through many of the songs Monroe wrote. Most were based on his true-life situations. His heart spoke often through his music.

"Blue Moon of Kentucky" has been recorded widely. Mentioned in an earlier chapter, Elvis Presley began his recording career with it and, in recent years, Paul McCartney paid respects with his acoustic rendition. Other laments include the up-tempo "Used To Be," while in "Walk Softly on My Heart," cowritten with Jake Landers, one can feel Monroe's anguish. His "True Life Blues" is filled with images of a home being broken apart. Regrets are expressed in the heartfelt "Can't You Hear Me Callin'."

It was not all sad for "Big Mon." Fond memories are evoked in "My Little Georgia Rose." The timeless "Uncle Pen" continues to capture the spirit of Pendleton Vandiver, the uncle whom Monroe worshipped and whose dance-driven fiddling he went on to share with the world as bluegrass music. When Monroe would perform this number, he typically broke into some fancy footsteps, completing the picture.

The instrumentals Monroe wrote are as thoughtfully constructed as any classical music piece. They exhibit sophistication as well as complexity. Take in "Raw Hide," "Scotland," "Roanoke," or "Blue Grass Breakdown," for example. Young players continue to try to break the sound barrier with speed on these and others. Longtime Blue Grass Boy, fiddler Kenny Baker recorded an album, *Kenny Baker Plays Bill Monroe*, on which he included such tunes as "Jerusalem Ridge," "Lonesome Moonlight Waltz," and "Brown County Breakdown."

Interesting to note are the songs that have been written *about* Bill Monroe, in addition to the many written about bluegrass music itself. It is a revealing aspect of the genre to find material written about its originator. Most were written during Monroe's lifetime, which is even more telling about the depth with which its practitioners feel the music and the influence of Monroe.

Legendary composers Felice and Boudleaux Bryant penned a salute to the "Father of Bluegrass" with "Daddy Bluegrass," while mandolinist Butch Baldassari tips his hat to "Big Mon" in "Waltz for Bill Monroe" as well as in "Happy Birthday, Bill Monroe," performed by his Nashville Mandolin Ensemble. The Nashville Bluegrass Band recorded the instrumental "Monroebillia," mandolinist Mike Compton's insightful contribution. Ireland's Niall Toner Band offers a tongue-in-cheek "Bill Monroe's Mandolin."

A statement on the state of traditional music in the face of rock-and-roll is made in Tom T. Hall's "Elvis on Velvet and Monroe on Grass," recorded by Gary Brewer and the Kentucky Ramblers. Hall wrote and sang another, "Bill Monroe for Breakfast," on *Home Grown*. Nashville's Clarence and Armolee Greene recorded "Legend of Bill Monroe," written by Bob Angle.

The Wildwood Valley Boys reminisce while mourning the passing of Bill Monroe in "The Big Man from Rosine," written by Aubrey Holt of Boys From Indiana fame. The lyrics are a beautifully crafted picture of the man and his music. On a memorial tribute CD, *My Father*, performer James

Monroe includes "Bean Blossom Memories," reflecting on the long-running annual festival his father established in that Indiana town.

In "The Cross-Eyed Child," John Hartford provides an epic part-personal reminiscence, part-biography as told to him by Monroe and others. He recounts conversations in which Monroe confided his fears when teased as a cross-eyed child and gave insight into the origin of his vocal style. The ten-and-a-half-minute accounting is mostly narrative rendered in Hartford's relaxed storytelling manner, filled out here and there with song. The final vignette Hartford relates is of Monroe in his hospital bed, still composing music even while nearing his last days. The song is not sad or mournful but rather conveys the determination and success of the musician and the man.

Although Bill Monroe wrote many a song, often steeped in heartbreak, he perhaps spoke best of himself through his numerous instrumentals, including "Monroe's Blues." His most telling, as well as compelling, tune is "My Last Days on Earth," where his mandolin speaks from his innermost soul.

The bluegrass theme or the word alone shows up in songs too many times to relate here. Since bluegrass contains integral elements of the blues, that word probably places a close second. Finally, the color blue likely comes in third. While the title is "Bluegrass Blues," the lyrics lead in as "blue, blue bluegrass blues," in a song found on a CD of the same name by Melvin Goins and Windy Mountain. It also can be heard on the self-titled *The Steep Canyon Rangers*.

The Stanley Brothers have given the bluegrass world countless originals, Carter's much loved "The White Dove" among them. Emmylou Harris gave an expressive rendition of Ralph's pensive "The Darkest Hour Is Just before Dawn" on her *Roses in the Snow* album.

Lester Flatt and Earl Scruggs also wrote many songs and tunes, some separately, others as a team. "Flint Hill Special," "Earl's Breakdown," and "Foggy Mountain Breakdown" are three best-loved instrumentals. "Down the Road," "My Cabin in Caroline," and "We'll Meet Again Sweetheart" are enduring songs performed by many.

Gospel songs figure into the mix as well. Not only are age-old hymns relied on but also new bluegrass gospel continues to be written. Bill Monroe penned one of the most moving, covered by many, the solemn "Get Down on Your Knees and Pray." From Flatt and Scruggs comes "God Loves His Children," filled with joyful spirit.

Albert E. Brumley, Sr. could be referred to as the granddaddy of gospel songwriting. He composed more than eight hundred bluegrass and country songs, primarily gospel. Many of his songs are known worldwide and are sung outside the realm of those two genres. Bob Dylan, Jerry Lee Lewis, the Brown's Ferry Four, and Elvis Presley have recorded his songs.

His most famous, "I'll Fly Away," has been recorded at least five hundred times in nearly every discipline, including classical. It gained renewed attention after being featured in *O Brother, Where Art Thou?*, albeit to occasional irreverent notice. In February 2004, the ABC television program *America's Funniest Home Videos* used the Alison Krauss–Gillian Welch rendition from the film to play behind footage of various mishaps that occurred during parasailing and wind sport activities. Perhaps the creators of an older television series starring Sam Waterston were inspired to title the program based on this Brumley song title.

Mac Wiseman popularized Brumley's "I'd Rather Live by the Side of the Road" in bluegrass in the 1950s. It was later recorded by the Seldom Scene and, more recently, by Eddie and Martha Adcock. His "Rank Strangers" is often heard in performance by Ralph Stanley, who recorded it with Carter in 1960. "Turn Your Radio On" remains popular, recorded by many including the McLain Family Band and John Hartford. The Johnson Mountain Boys have recorded live a rousing rendition of his "I've Found a Hiding Place," which exhibits amazing vocal acrobatics that lend to the power of the song.

One of the most prolific bluegrass songwriters has been Pete Goble, whose career spans the entire life, to date, of the music. His songs have been recorded and performed by such artists as Jimmy Martin, the Osborne Brothers, Larry Sparks, Eddie Adcock Band, Country Gentlemen, Hot Rize, Lynn Morris Band, country singer Marty Robbins, and dozens of others.

With frequent collaborator Leroy Drumm, among his best-known titles are "Blue Virginia Blues," "Tennessee 1949," "Walking the Blues," and "Coleen Malone." This last was most recently popularized by Larry Sparks as well as by Tim O'Brien's rendition with Hot Rize. Goble has also penned with Bobby Osborne such songs as "This Heart of Mine (Can Never Say Goodbye)," "I'll Be Alright Tomorrow," and "Big Spike Hammer."

In October 2002, Goble was honored by the International Bluegrass Music Association with its Lifetime Achievement Award. We spent a few minutes after the awards ceremony in Louisville, Kentucky, chatting about songwriting, his long career, and bluegrass music. I asked Goble what special quality bluegrass songs have that set them apart, what makes a bluegrass song special?

> It's got a feeling to it; it's unique. It brings a message out and it's got a good driving beat. Music to me, all music that's good, has got a drive to it. If it's slow, it's still got a certain kind of drive to it. And if it's fast, the drive is there, too. Of course, it's in the eye of the beholder, but what I listen to is a good beat to a song.
>
> I like to leave people with a message. For instance, I had never seen *The Lone Ranger* (radio program) in my life when I was a kid, but I *rode* with him as a kid, you know, on the radio. That's the best way I can explain it. If I sing it like Tom T. Hall—that's my hero—when he writes a song and he sings it, you can feel it. You just see the character in the song. Each song he writes, it's like you've seen a movie.

Often considered his signature song, "Your Old Standby" was written by Jim Eanes. He composed and recorded many memorable songs that continue to be renewed time and again by younger artists. "Baby Blue Eyes" and "I Wouldn't Change You If I Could," a number one hit for Ricky Skaggs on the country charts in the 1980s, are two of his widely recognized numbers. One of his best-selling songs was the gospel "In His Arms I'm Not Afraid," recorded in the late sixties.

Randall Hylton ranks in the top spectrum of all-time great bluegrass songwriters. His many compositions could fill a volume. Before his 2001 death, he had experienced great success with such titles as "Slippers with Wings," "Keep the Candles Burning," "Oh, Anita," and "Room at the Top of the Stairs." His topics ran the gamut, from gospel to humor to love, and his works have been covered by scores of artists, including Charlie Waller, Larry Stephenson, the Adcocks, Special Consensus, the Lewis Family, David Parmley and Continental Divide, and the Rarely Herd.

Several women songwriters figure prominently in songs associated with Bill Monroe. Such numbers as "I Live in the Past," "Road of Life," and "With Body and Soul" were written by Virginia Stauffer. Also for Monroe, Hazel Smith, a well-known country music writer, penned "Thank God for Kentucky." Her sons, Billy and Terry Smith, are among Nashville's most prominent songwriters. The Smith brothers' "A Deeper Shade of Blue" was the title cut of the Del McCoury Band's award-winning CD.

Hazel Dickens is one of the most beloved singer-songwriters in bluegrass who also crosses boundaries with her traditional and folk-style material. She has been a moving force among contemporary social protest songwriters, laying out, in particular, the plight of the West Virginia coal-mining communities. Four of Dickens's songs appear on the soundtrack of the Academy Award–winning documentary *Harlan County, USA*. The John Sayles film *Matewan*, also about the coal-mining camps, features Dickens's persuasive voice on several numbers.

In the late sixties, early seventies, she and Alice Gerrard recorded two albums of primarily bluegrass songs, gaining prominence for women with lead voices in bluegrass settings. Her more recent solo recordings showcase her thought-provoking, spirited compositions as well as the conviction in her powerful delivery. Her song "Mama's Hand" took the IBMA Song of the Year award in 1996, as recorded by the Lynn Morris Band.

Further mention of John Hartford is in order here. He had an enormous range of material that he penned. Most could not be faithfully categorized as bluegrass; yet, it merits repeating that he and his music reached out to erase lines between genres. It is well worth investigating his many recordings to explore his originality and his perspective of bluegrass and other traditional music.

Paul Craft is a household name in bluegrass and country songbooks. First surfacing with modest success in the late sixties, Craft has consistently pulled out winners since that time. Linda Ronstadt and the Seldom Scene put "Keep Me from Blowin' Away" on the map. Alison Krauss recorded "Teardrops Will Kiss the Morning Dew," included on *Now That I've Found You.* "Drop Kick Me Jesus" is memorable in the country music world. The Eagles, the Lewis Family, J.J. Cale, and Jerry Lee Lewis are just a hint of the countless artists who have recorded his songs.

Larry Cordle represents today's successful clique of writers that also includes such fine younger composers as Chris Brashear and Donna Hughes. Cordle has garnered numerous awards, including several for "Murder on Music Row," a swipe at the country music industry for pushing aside its roots, cowritten with Larry Shell and recorded in duet by country stars George Strait and Alan Jackson. Others he has cowritten have been recorded widely in country and bluegrass, including by Garth Brooks, Reba McEntire, George Jones, Alison Krauss, and Ricky Skaggs.

A wordsmith with a knack for "perfect country song titles,"—"Lost as a Ball in High Weeds" is one recent success—Cordle showcases his songs with his award-winning bluegrass group, Larry Cordle and Lonesome Standard Time. I caught up with Cordle at a festival during Labor Day weekend in 2003 and inquired whether he writes with a particular sound in mind, since many of his originals cross over.

"I was raised around bluegrass," he responded. "They would refer to me as 'that bluegrass guy.' I write more bluesy than some, but my mom encouraged me to do my own thing. You know, it's simply that good songs are also timeless."

Cordle went on to explain that one of his earlier successful songs, "The Fields of Home," is "like my childhood and the way I was raised, true as anything I ever wrote. Lyrically, it is as much me as anything." This longing, love, and respect for home and family continues to prevail in contemporary bluegrass songs, not much differently from songs written five and six decades ago.

Tim O'Brien is a versatile performer and songwriter. A member of Hot Rize and leader of his own bands, he smoothly glides into any number of musical settings in his playing and singing, from bluegrass and traditional to swing and country. He manages the same in his exceptional songwriting. Those who have covered his material include the Dixie Chicks, Garth Brooks, Laurie Lewis, New Grass Revival, Nickel Creek, and Kathy Mattea.

Chris Jones is known primarily as a singer, fronting his own group as well as his previous affiliations with such bands as Weary Hearts and Special Consensus. His originals encompass the emotional swings triggered by love, life challenges, hardships, and tragedy. His sensitive "A Few Words," for example, is deeply personal—about the loss of his mother—but conveys feelings possessed by all. Two well-known songs from Chris's pen are "Dark Wind of Missouri" and "Blinded by the Rose."

Even before he started his own band, River Bend, in 1978, Dave Evans was already turning heads. He first began to leave his mark singing and playing banjo with such artists as Larry Sparks, Red Allen, the Boys From Indiana, and the Goins Brothers. His voice stands out for its dramatic expression, covering others' as well as his own compositions. First recorded in 1981, "One Loaf of Bread" remains superbly representative of songs from the pen of this socially aware, prolific songwriter.

Others, bastions and relative newcomers alike, whose songs are often found in the bluegrass catalog include Harley Allen (son of "Red" Allen), Ronnie Bowman, Pam Gadd, John Herald, Carl Jackson, Kathy Kallick, Laurie Lewis, Claire Lynch, John Pennell, Phil Rosenthal, Peter Rowan, Jimmie Skinner, Chris Stuart, Wayne Taylor, as well as the legendary Halls, Tom T. and Dixie.

SONGS FOR THE YOUNG 'UNS

Numerous bluegrass groups or solo artists perform children-specific material. It is not necessarily "pure" bluegrass and generally hinges on folk and other forms yet is played on typically bluegrass instruments or in a bluegrass style. Doc Watson recorded a CD called *Doc Watson Sings Songs for Little Pickers Live!* Cathy Fink and Marcy Marxer also perform and record an eclectic collection of children's material, as does Phil Rosenthal, former lead singer with the Seldom Scene. He does an extensive amount of work focused on children. Kathy Kallick as well as David Holt, whose music hovers between old-time and bluegrass, both have recordings devoted to music aimed at children. Rhonda Vincent recorded "Bananaphone" for Putumayo World Music's CD, *Sing Along With Putumayo.*

GIVING VOICE TO THE SONGS

Now that you have been introduced to some of the songwriters and songs, the picture would not be complete without mentioning examples of the most recognizable and distinctive vocalists. There are many powerful voices out there on the bluegrass circuit, some of whom have been talked about in earlier chapters. The lead singers have a punch and drive not readily found in other genres. Supporting musicians are just as intricately woven into the mix. Trio and quartet harmony singing, especially in a cappella situations, brings everyone into the vocal spotlight.

Here are a handful of names, not mentioned previously for their vocal abilities, to listen for: Ronnie Bowman, Dale Ann Bradley, Paul Brewster, Kathy Chiavola, Honi Deaton, Pat Enright, Kim Fox, Jim Hurst, Sally Jones, Dwight McCall, Lynn Morris, Mark Newton, Michelle Nixon, Alan O'Bryant, James Reams, Lou Reid, Don Rigsby, Peter Rowan, Amanda Smith, Valerie Smith, Martha Trachtenberg, Doc Watson, Danny Weiss.

JIM LAUDERDALE: LOST IN THE PINES
WITH RALPH STANLEY

Best known for his dynamic vocals in country music and often heard on the *Grand Ole Opry*, Jim Lauderdale has more recently been recognized for his side trips in bluegrass, writing, recording, and performing with Ralph Stanley. Originally from North Carolina, Lauderdale is among the cream of the crop of contemporary songwriters but who also knows well how to create a song "in the tradition."

George Strait, Patty Loveless, and George Jones join countless artists who have recorded Lauderdale material. Among his cowriters is Robert Hunter, who was Jerry Garcia's writing partner.

On *I Feel Like Singing Today*, Jim Lauderdale and Ralph Stanley explore the colorful images of the people about whom bluegrass is sung. They delved again into a rich catalog of traditional and originals when they teamed up for *Lost in the Lonesome Pines*, which took home Grammy honors in 2003. On these two collaborative recordings, they cover songs Carter and Ralph Stanley brought into the bluegrass tradition, as well as brand new compositions that Lauderdale now introduces with Ralph into the new tradition.

SPL: How do you make a new song old, that is to carry on the tradition of bluegrass songs that were written forty years ago?

JL: That's a good question. In the case with the things I did with Ralph Stanley and the Clinch Mountain Boys, I knew that Ralph had his own particular style that he and Carter developed and Ralph has carried on. So, when I was writing for the record, I couldn't stray too far from that style. That was a challenge. Luckily I had listened to a lot of Stanley Brothers when I was a kid, so I had a feel for Ralph. That is what helped me do that.

I kind of had writer's block while I was writing for both of those records. I had cowritten several songs with people who also—and this was a big help— people who were very versed in the Stanley sound. Robert Hunter, oddly enough, who, well, not oddly enough, he and Jerry Garcia both were big Ralph Stanley fans. So he was familiar, very familiar with Ralph, and he gave me several sets of lyrics. Ollie O'Shea also was very familiar with Ralph. Candace Randolph has had [songs recorded by] Ralph Stanley. Her family is old friends of Ralph's and she grew up listening to Ralph. And Shawn Camp who is a great bluegrass artist and writer.

With these cowriters, they had this familiarity. Then the stuff that I wrote alone for Ralph, I kind of just thought about him a lot. I couldn't finish several of the lyrics until the very last minute in the studio. I had to have that pressure on me. And it was very daunting, because I had Ralph Stanley and his band waiting in the other room, and I had to stall 'em while I would go in the other room and finish something. Luckily they knew what was going on; they're very understanding. Ralph said that at several Stanley Brothers sessions, Carter would have to go in the other room and finish a song. He was used to that in a way.

Some of my other bluegrass songs don't fit that Stanley sound, but they're still bluegrass. Now I feel like there's kind of a bridge between traditional country, traditional bluegrass, and some of this newer stuff I'm writing.

SPL: When you write, do you aim to write in the style of a particular genre, or do you just write and let the melody and lyrics come out and fall where the chips may?

JL: Yes, I like that. I usually get the melodies first anyway, maybe the title, and then the melody will come from the title. It's more fun for me when songs just come out. It seems over the last several years, I've always had some project or another in the works. I do kind of very eclectic records. I guess you call them progressive country or singer-songwriter records. I try to do a regular traditional country record in that cycle, because I feel like it's kind of a dying folk art in a way. So I wanna kind of do that every few years or so, just to keep things going, do songs in that vein of writing, but make it new, to try not to repeat too many of the same lyrics or themes that have already been written, because everything really has already been written. My goal is to just try to do something that's a little bit unique.

SPL: Given the standard topics of love, home, etc., what new topics should bluegrass be exploring in the twenty-first century, while remaining fresh and still being bluegrass?

JL: Everybody is still going to do love songs, because those are, in every field of music, just about, that's the predominant theme. So that'll keep happening. There will still be sad songs and there will still be gospel songs in bluegrass. Probably some of the more progressive bands will be doing quirky things that we didn't think of. "Oh boy, I never heard anybody try that before." I think there will be new themes coming along, too.

SPL: Whom did you look up to in bluegrass as a songwriter?

JL: Monroe, of course, Carter Stanley, Ralph. When I was in high school, I also listened to the Seldom Scene and the Country Gentlemen, who were doing songs by contemporary songwriters. And Tony Rice, who would do, like, Gordon Lightfoot songs. The Seldom Scene—I kind of almost discovered Rodney Crowell through them. I look up to songwriters like Gram Parsons and Harlan Howard and other country songwriters who [took] a lot of the older bluegrass and [were] converting the modern country songs at the time, the bluegrass that really fit well. I think that will happen probably more and more today as well.

SPL: Who do you think are the up-and-coming bluegrass songwriters to watch for?

JL: This fellow I mentioned before, Shawn Camp. I think he is really going to start exploding with the new stuff. And I think people ought to keep their eyes out for Ralph Stanley II, because he is one of the most enthusiastic young songwriters I've run across. Every time I see him, he's got a new song started that he wants to play for me. He just lives and breathes music, bluegrass and country music. And he is a real authority on it at a real young age. Also there's a woman I've written with I mentioned, Candace Randolph; I think she's going to be coming out with more and more stuff, too.

Interview conducted September 30, 2003, World of Bluegrass Trade Show, Galt House, Louisville, Kentucky.

"Father of Bluegrass" Bill Monroe performing at the Lincoln Center Out-of-Doors Festival, New York City, August 23, 1987.

Banjo innovator Earl Scruggs, with Glen Duncan on fiddle (background), appearing at the Count Basie Theatre, Red Bank, New Jersey, October 24, 2002.

Karl Shiflett and Big Country Show entertaining at the 2002 Delaware Valley Bluegrass Festival, Woodstown, New Jersey.

Nashville Bluegrass Band harmonizing with the Fairfield Four, 3rd Annual International Bluegrass Music Association Awards Show, RiverPark Center, Owensboro, Kentucky, September 24, 1992.

Del McCoury with Mike Bub on bass, appearing Labor Day Weekend 2002, Delaware Valley Bluegrass Festival, Woodstown, New Jersey.

Mountain Heart performs at the 13th Annual International Bluegrass Music Association Awards Show, Kentucky Center for the Arts, Louisville, Kentucky, October 17, 2002.

Alison Krauss and Alison Brown in an early Union Station performance at the Philadelphia Bluegrass Festival, March 9, 1990.

"King of Bluegrass" Jimmy Martin on stage with Audie Blaylock (mandolin) and Chris Warner (banjo). Waterloo Bluegrass Festival, Stanhope, New Jersey, August 23, 1986.

Ralph Stanley signing autographs at his CD sales table, Delaware Valley Bluegrass Festival, Salem County Fairgrounds, Woodstown, New Jersey, Labor Day Weekend 2003.

Nickel Creek's Chris Thile, Philadelphia Folk Festival, August 25, 2001.

Sweden's Downhill Bluegrass Band rehearsing before taking to the stage to greet fans at the Delaware Valley Bluegrass Festival, Woodstown, New Jersey, August 30, 2003.

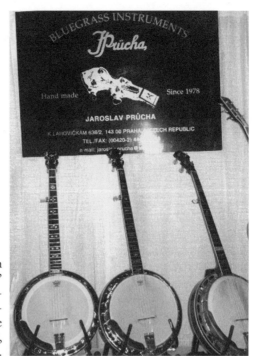

Banjos made in the Czech Republic by Jaroslav "Jerry" Prücha, on display at the International Bluegrass Music Association World of Bluegrass Trade Show, Louisville, Kentucky, October 2003.

Campground jam session at the 2003 Delaware Valley Bluegrass Festival, Salem County Fairgrounds, Woodstown, New Jersey. In the foreground is a fire containment drum for campsite cooking. Barbecue feasts among friends and picking neighbors are part of the fun at festivals.

New kid on the block: Sierra Hull at age eleven, Louisville, Kentucky, October 2002.

Lynn Morris Band in a Hunterdon County, New Jersey Parks Department concert, June 2001.

Young pickers warm up backstage at the Bluegrass Fan Fest, Louisville, Kentucky, October 2002. From left to right, Maggie Beth Estes, fiddle (back to camera); Jennifer Kennedy, dobro; Tyler Andal, fiddle; Nic Andal, guitar; unidentified bass and banjo players.

Doc Watson and David Grisman, Grand Opera House, Wilmington, Delaware, October 24, 1998.

John McEuen of the
Nitty Gritty Dirt Band.
Count Basie Theatre,
Red Bank, New Jersey,
October 24, 2002.

Bluegrass merges with classical and jazz on the "Short Trip Home" project featuring
(left to right) Mike Marshall, Joshua Bell, Edgar Meyer, and Sam Bush. McCarter
Theatre, Princeton, New Jersey, October 25, 1999.

"Women in Bluegrass" performance at the 10th Annual International Bluegrass Music Awards, Palace Theater, Louisville, Kentucky, October 21, 1999. From left, Claire Lynch, Missy Raines, Rhonda Vincent, Laurie Lewis, Lynn Morris.

Everett Lilly, of the Lilly Brothers, appearing at the Delaware Valley Bluegrass Festival, Salem County Fairgrounds, Woodstown, New Jersey, Labor Day Weekend 2003.

Little Roy Lewis cuts up during a set by Buck White and the Down Home Folks (now known as The Whites). (L-R) Buck White, Little Roy, Sharon White, Mark Hembree. McLain Family Festival, Berea, Kentucky, August 15, 1982.

Béla Fleck with New Grass Revival, March 27, 1985, Lone Star Café, New York City.

Stacy Phillips plays dobro alongside Jimmy Arnold (obscured) on guitar. New York City Bluegrass Festival, Snug Harbor, Staten Island, New York, June 30, 1985.

Ricky Skaggs and Kentucky Thunder perform at the 13th Annual International Bluegrass Music Association Awards Show, Kentucky Center for the Arts, Louisville, Kentucky, October 17, 2002.

7

Popular Culture: Got Bluegrass?

Got bluegrass? Seems lots of people are getting bluegrass of late. There is even a term for it, the "O Brother phenomenon." That's right; it's a phenomenon.

The "O Brother phenomenon," or "effect," has been and continues to be talked about, written about, opined about in everything from music publications to online discussion groups, academic seminars, and the *New York Times*. This effect is very likely the reason you are reading this book. Got bluegrass? It sure looks that way, or at least you are on the road to getting it.

As I touched on in the Introduction, a number of factors propelled the music from the film into the spotlight and into the public's ears. The "O Brother effect" is that bluegrass is benefiting—on a large scale—from the exposure the film and its soundtrack gave it and other related roots musics. Popularity has increased, the primary gauge of which is CD sales within the whole bluegrass genre, not sales of the soundtrack alone. The Simmons survey, mentioned at the beginning of the book, tallied a doubling of consumers buying bluegrass recordings from the year 2000, which was before the release of *O Brother*, to the year 2003, well into the midst of the "O Brother phenomenon."

Worth repeating is that the sales of this pivotal soundtrack are astounding. Six-and-a-half-million units had been sold by the end of 2003, according to data collected by Nielsen SoundScan.[1] It is also interesting to note

[1]Nielsen SoundScan is an information system that tracks sales of music and music video products throughout the United States and Canada. Sales data from point-of-sale cash registers are collected weekly from over 14,000 retail, mass merchant, and nontraditional (online stores, venues, etc.) outlets. Nielsen SoundScan is the sales source for the *Billboard* music charts, http://www.soundscan.com/about.html.

that, in a casual check of a major online retailer on March 4, 2004, a little more than three years since its initial release, the *O Brother, Where Art Thou?* CD showed a sales ranking at eighty-seven—out of thousands of available products. To sustain such sales might not be unusual for, say, Britney Spears or the Beatles, but bluegrass? That's a phenomenon.

No, not many bluegrass artists are getting rich quick, if at all or if ever! Unfortunately, bluegrass remains what is called a nonmainstream music, you know, one that the "big guys" generally don't support. Corporations, which in these times are the majority owners of commercial radio stations around the country, generally do not permit such music on their stations. In their financial eyes, bluegrass is not commercially viable enough to sell the amount of advertising dollars they require to remain operational and to remain, well, the big guys.

The "O Brother effect" has pervaded our lives in another way and gives further credence to its being a phenomenon. Since the tumult began, numerous headlines have appeared in magazines, newspapers, in advertising, in titles of other recordings that play off the catch phrase "O Brother." Many of these have had little, if anything, to do with the film or the music.

A print ad for the Ozark Folk Center in Mountain View, Arkansas, proclaims, "Oh [*sic*] Brother, Here We Are! ...Been Here All Along." Spotted in a magazine was a quote from the editor of a new music publication aimed at the over-thirty set in which he refers to that audience as the "*Oh* [*sic*] *Brother Where Art Thou* crowd." Discussing the state of bluegrass, *USA Weekend* posed "O Bluegrass, Where Art Thou Headed?" in a January 2002 edition. From Disney comes a CD, *O Mickey, Where Art Thou?*, on which several leading bluegrass musicians are heard backing name country stars in a bluegrass-country presentation of Disney hits. Finally, the Peasall Sisters, heard in the *O Brother* and *Down from the Mountain* projects, are one of several lending talent to bluegrass and country gospel on *O Veggie, Where Art Thou?* from Veggie Tales.

Suffice it to say there are numerous indicators that show bluegrass and related genres are getting more exposure worldwide, gaining in popularity, and seeping more and more into our daily lives. Wait, what do I mean "more and more"? Yes, that's right; it's been here all along. Whether you noticed it at an earlier time or not, we all pretty much "got" bluegrass at some point in our lives before this "O Brother phenomenon" let loose. Go back to my Introduction; you will see I have mentioned any number of television programs, commercials, and movies from thirty and forty years ago. I will talk about that with additional interesting tidbits in a few minutes. First, let's look at another, earlier "phenomenon," the "Circle effect."

MUSIC FORMS A NEW CIRCLE

The impetus for writing *Homegrown Music: Discovering Bluegrass* was the unprecedented success of the music from *O Brother, Where Art Thou?* and the subsequent surge in popularity for bluegrass. However, an earlier defining event kicked bluegrass and traditional country music into gear more than thirty years ago. Its impact was of tremendous significance then and rings true especially today, as legions of new fans of bluegrass and roots music turn their attention back in time to pure American-made music.

In 1970, the Nitty Gritty Dirt Band was known as an eclectic, if not eccentric, folk-rock band, whose music took many twists and turns. The group forayed into country sounds, fiddle and banjo tunes, gentle folk-style ballads, and even classical music played on banjo. It had hit the pop charts with "Buy for Me the Rain" in the mid-sixties, followed by a smash hit with Jerry Jeff Walker's "Mr. Bojangles" in 1970. Back then the members also had a dream.

Will the Circle Be Unbroken was a concept ahead of its time. Multi-instrumentalist John McEuen had an idea, which was then put into play by brother William McEuen, the Nitty Gritty Dirt Band's producer. The group was paving the way for country-rock, then in its infancy, in its sound. Now there was the desire to authenticate the roots of that innovative, roots-oriented approach. The band wanted to bring together its lifelong bluegrass and country music heroes to record an album. It was unprecedented to gather such a stellar cast of musical figures in one recording studio.

With a nod of approval from the musically open-minded Earl and Louise Scruggs, who helped open the door to other notables, the band was able to persuade nearly all the legends and major players of bluegrass and traditional country music to participate. The roster included Scruggs, "Mother" Maybelle Carter, Doc Watson, Roy Acuff, guitar stylist Merle Travis, Jimmy Martin, Vassar Clements, Junior Huskey, Norman Blake, and Pete "Oswald" Kirby (Bashful Brother Oswald). The only one missing was Bill Monroe, who declined, reportedly not wanting to be associated with any form of rock music. Vinyl still being the standard playback medium back then, the result was a three-record set.

In its first month after release in 1972, *Will the Circle Be Unbroken* had already sold 25,000 copies, tremendous figures in those days, especially considering that the album retailed for triple the usual price. A promotional postcard referred to it as "a runaway, and largely unexpected, success." Clearly this is similar to the "phenomenon" witnessed with the music from *O Brother, Where Art Thou?* in recent years.

Bear in mind, technology then was nothing like what exists now. Communication for dissemination of publicity was limited. Retail sales certainly did not have the benefit of "online" outlets. Even radio and television broadcasting, which influences exposure and popularity, did not come close to today's possibilities.

If that same album had been released in the twenty-first century, with all the current forms of sharing information as well as the music itself, results might very well have been much like that which occurred with the *O Brother* music. Nevertheless, the impact of the *Circle* recording was significant, introducing bluegrass to a new audience comprised of rock, folk, and country fans. The success of both pivotal albums demonstrated that there was an audience for bluegrass and traditional music; the music simply needed the right vehicle to reach out and touch that segment of the population.

Rereleased in 2002 in celebration of its thirty-year anniversary, the original *Will the Circle Be Unbroken* continues to win accolades and to bring notice to the music and its many notable musicians, some who are no longer around to enjoy its renewed and expanded popularity. Two similar follow-up CDs were also released with an updated lineup of legends and current celebrities, *Will the Circle Be Unbroken, Volume II* (1989) and *Volume III* (2002), although neither gained the momentum of the original in spite of all-star casts.

WHY NOW?

One can speculate as to why bluegrass seems to be coming into its own and holding its own at this time. There are numerous choices in music today, especially with the global ability of the Internet to bring music instantly to one's personal space. In light of real-life violence and turmoil going on around us, as well as that reflected in some popular music, family values and a back-to-basics attitude have taken on new significance.

The movie *O Brother, Where Art Thou?* was not a runaway success, yet the music featured in it was. Let's examine that scenario for a moment. The film was an interpretative retelling of Homer's *The Odyssey*, the complex adventure that follows the trials and tribulations of a crafty chieftain returning home to Ithaca after the ten-year Trojan War. Along the way, Odysseus is faced with a number of physically and emotionally challenging as well as dangerous situations. He suffers—and learns—a lot but, in the outcome, arrives home and is reunited with his family.

The Coen Brothers' colorful take on the arduous journey is set in the 1930's Deep South, Mississippi, with Odysseus portrayed as a prisoner on the lam trying to make it back to his family. His quest is fraught with the dangers of the times, from unscrupulous businessmen to the Ku Klux Klan.

Along the way, he and his pals, a.k.a. the Soggy Bottom Boys, stumble into a successful music career; they cut a record that results in an unexpected hit song. Moreover, the song's content speaks to hardships they endured.

The music employed in the movie beautifully and aptly illustrates each scene, be it humorous, romantic, or in-your-face death. The simplicity of the music and its intelligent and appropriate use depicting specific scenes facilitate the movement of each sequence. The film is as much a reflection of today's trying times as it was of Ulysses Everett McGill's (George Clooney); in the end, warm and fuzzy music accompanies a triumphant homecoming and reuniting with family.

Members of the bluegrass media, its artists, and others involved saw the film for its potential value in publicizing the music. It was a good—an excellent—product, which they ran with, setting into motion timely marketing. Word went out; fans heard about it, talked it up, bought the CD soundtrack, and told others about it. Momentum built and, before long, mainstream media took notice. The rest, as they say, is history.

Certainly, a major contributing factor has been the Internet and the World Wide Web. Since the late sixties, the Internet, a vast internationally-connected computer network, was used mainly in academia and military settings for research and communications. However, that began to change with the establishment in 1989 of the World Wide Web, which introduced and created new ways for graphics and multimedia files to be viewed, heard, and shared via the Internet. The opportunities to hear music from just about any corner of the Earth are seemingly endless as a result. When the *Circle* album released in 1972, this vehicle was not yet at hand.

BEYOND O BROTHER

Musicians themselves are latching on to the "O Brother phenomenon" in another manner. Many are collaborating on recordings and appearances with artists from other genres. Others are returning to the bluegrass fold.

As already mentioned, classical and bluegrass first met long ago. In recent years, mandolinist Butch Baldassari created his "Orchestral Celebration of the Music of Bill Monroe," a five-movement work that chronicles the music of and pays tribute to the "Father of Bluegrass" as well as to his mentor, Uncle Pen.

Irish traditional music is well established as a natural complementary genre. The Chieftains' *Plank Road* Nashville sessions are exemplary. From Canada, Cape Breton's acclaimed fiddler Natalie MacMaster enlisted several bluegrass luminaries on *Blueprint*. Even multiple Grammy winner Norah Jones was noted by a newspaper reviewer to have "added some bluegrass flavor" to a number during a 2003 concert.

The quirky Peter Schickele in his P.D.Q. Bach incarnation performed Baroque backed by a bluegrass band that included Eric Weissberg, Bill Keith, and Happy Traum. Traum played banjo alongside Bob Dylan on Dylan's *Greatest Hits, Volume II*. Dylan, of course, has dabbled in bluegrass and other traditional sounds over the years.

Several major country and pop-folk artists have embraced or returned to their roots during their careers, including Michelle Shocked, Patty Loveless, and Dolly Parton. Country star Vince Gill got his start playing in several bluegrass bands and often is heard guesting on bluegrass efforts.

GOT BLUEGRASS? COMMERCIAL EXPOSURE

In July 2003, I was pulling into my driveway, a local talk show in progress on my car radio. What I heard convinced me that bluegrass really had been here all along; most of us just did not realize it.

Film and television star Buddy Ebsen had just passed away. He portrayed "Jed Clampett" in *The Beverly Hillbillies* series of the sixties. The talk show host was conducting his daily TV theme song trivia contest, in which correct answers win listeners movie tickets. In tribute to Ebsen, he asked caller-contenders to sing the theme from *The Beverly Hillbillies.* What floored me was how many people called in and not only sang but also actually knew all the words to "The Ballad of Jed Clampett."

This little glimpse of bluegrass had broken through the far reaches of many a memory bank. Whether those callers knew the music they had heard on the comedy show was bluegrass, it is hard to say. Nevertheless, what is evident is that the music stuck with them.

Now, true, the song might not be the most representative of the big picture of bluegrass, but it is a part of that fabric. Other earlier television programs, including *The Andy Griffith Show* mentioned previously, had also featured bluegrass and traditional music occasionally. Before the Dillards became the Darling Boys on that show, the Kentucky Colonels filmed two episodes. Roland White was drafted into the military, so the Dillards ended up portraying the musical hillbilly sons.

During a conversation we had in October 2003, White recalled the humor that took place on and off the set. "We went to the cafeteria [for lunch] and there was Andy [Griffith] and Don Knotts [Barney Fife]," White began. "They were going over the sketch, the dialogue. Andy would do something and Don would say, 'Well, that's not what that says,' and they'd just laugh. They went on and on for like fifteen minutes. They had to go by the script, but they could improvise because they were able to. Not all of it but quite a bit of it."

White went on to provide this insight into Griffith's musical abilities: "Andy, he was wonderful," White stated. "Andy was very good on the guitar. He played with plastic picks. He played with us in the episode. We were backing him up. He's a good player, old-time style of playing."

Tennessee Ernie Ford made a handful of guest appearances on the original *I Love Lucy* show. One episode featured spirited fiddle-playing musicians on screen accompanying a jailbreak square dance. In another, as "Ernie Ford and His Four Hot Chicken Peckers," he leads Lucy, Ricky, Ethel, and Fred in a rousing rendition of the then relatively new song, "Y'all Come."

Public television continues to air an exciting diversity of programs related to bluegrass, folk, and roots music. The cover from the soundtrack of the documentary *High Lonesome: The Story of Bluegrass Music* was pictured on the front page of the *New York Times* television guide, promoting "Country Is Cool Week" on a cable network. In 1972, *The Wonderful World of Disney* aired *The Nashville Coyote*, which featured an on-demand band that included fiddle great Vassar Clements, dobro pioneer Tut Taylor, and multi-instrumentalist Norman Blake, to name a few. They performed "You Can't Go in the Red Playing Bluegrass," written for the movie.

In addition to those products or advertisers mentioned in the Introduction, numerous car and cereal makers seem to have an affinity for selling product with lively banjo or mandolin melodies. Competing salad dressings as well as SUVs duked it out to "Dueling Banjos" during 2003 television commercials. One of the country's largest banks played up its virtues to the tune of newgrass mandolin music. Twangy dobro is heard on segments of *This Old House*, while banjos ring out whenever Bob Barker tries to give away camping or fishing equipment on *The Price Is Right*.

Actor John Lithgow was shown with his banjo in a series of television commercials some years ago for Discover Card. More recently, Kelly Ripa told of having had banjo lessons as a child when Steve Martin was a guest on ABC's *Live with Regis and Kelly*, where he picked a tune or two to the obvious delight of the audience.

Any number of films have been popping up of late that are reaching back to basics with bluegrass and other roots music, following the lead set by the Coen Brothers and T Bone Burnett. The Coens and Burnett, too, continue to produce movies with a variety of traditional, gospel, and blues music, as they had done even before *O Brother*. Among those that have appeared in recent years are *Songcatcher*, *Cold Mountain*, and *Bell Witch, The Movie*.

Several news and news feature programs continue to give bluegrass its just due, among them ABC's *Nightline* as well as *World News Tonight with Peter Jennings* (who is a bluegrass fan), and *CBS News Sunday Morning* with host Charles Osgood, also a fan as well as a picker. A July 4, 2002, ABC special focused entirely on roots music from around the country, including bluegrass. There could not be a better time for bluegrass; as Americans, we identify with it.

CIRCLE OF TRADITION: NITTY GRITTY DIRT BAND

Thirty years after the original release of the influential *Will the Circle Be Unbroken* recording, I had the opportunity to reflect on its impact with two members of the Nitty Gritty Dirt Band, John McEuen and Jeff Hanna. For me, personally, it was completing my own full circle. My first introduction to bluegrass was in the fall of 1970 when I heard the group's music on the *Uncle Charlie and His Dog Teddy* recording as well as in two local concerts the Nitty Gritty Dirt Band gave. While I had met and seen John as a solo artist many times since those earliest encounters, this was my first opportunity in nearly thirty years to see the band.

SPL: John, why do you think the original *Circle* album had the impact it did thirty years ago?

JM: One reason it had the impact is the great music that's on it. The audience was there; they just didn't know where the music was. And because we were kind of on this flagship of notoriety with "Mr. Bojangles," "House at Pooh Corner," "Some of Shelley's Blues" getting played off the *Uncle Charlie* album that our audience looked at it. Attention got called to it. And when people heard the music, the word spread. In college dorms, wherever it was being played, people said, "What's that? I like that," or they said things like, "I don't even like that kind of music, but I like *that*!"

SPL: What makes the music so timeless and enduring?

JM: I think that's a question for the people listening to answer. Because all we're doing is trying to play things that we feel very natural about. On *Circle Vol. III*, the artists that were those guests were told, "Bring in a song you've wanted to record and that maybe doesn't fit on your own albums, or you've missed it, or something you're close to." The difference here was, most of the people on *Circle Vol. III*, including ourselves, grew up with the first one.

We made the first one, but we were way beyond our current level of understanding of that music. But you put us in that room with those people and it was an intensive crash course for a week, followed by the next ten years of listening to it, off and on, or playing the music on stage. And finding out that Sam Bush, Vince Gill, Ricky Skaggs, and Rodney Dillard—even though I started playing *because* of Rodney Dillard—even he listened to it. So we all knew what mark we had to hit and knew that there's a certain type of material it fit. Maybe it was a plaintive or it was a religious song without pointing at a particular religion, just a gospel tune, as they would call it. So, I think it was just a mutual effort of trying to have things that fit.

SPL: Tell me about the role bluegrass music has played in the planning of the three *Circle* recordings as well as with the career of the Nitty Gritty Dirt Band.

JM: Well, thanks to Rodney Dillard and Doug, who started a group called the Dillards that inspired me to play the banjo and get into music, I then came into the Dirt Band with the ideas of mandolins, banjos, and acoustic guitar stuff being part of the music. ... Jeff and Jimmie liked singing together. So, they'd find the songs that fit that form. We've never said the *Circle Be Unbroken* albums are bluegrass, 'cause they aren't really. But they're partially bluegrass. Even though they aren't necessarily bluegrass, the influence is there. It's hard to cut a country record with electric instruments without a steel guitar that's influenced by some of the early steel players. 'Cause bluegrass, as laid down by the masters, the creators, is often much broader than current people want to admit. 'Cause anybody that tells me Don Reno doesn't fit into bluegrass is wrong. People have said that over the years. Or Eddie Adcock, he fit in to Don Reno style of bluegrass. On the other hand, you know, Ralph Stanley says it's all country music.

SPL: Who is the audience for the *Circle* albums?

JM: I think in the early years it was a lot of college dropouts from other parts of music, not college dropouts, but musical dropouts. Doctors, lawyers, Indian chiefs, a variety of people, as well as people that are familiar with the sources of that music… in other words, real aficionados of old-timey.

SPL: Has each successive *Circle* album generated not just a lot of new fans, but a lot of new pickers?

JM: Definitely. I'm constantly running into people who say they started playing because of it. One of my favorite fiddle players is Phil Salazar out in California. And Phil will say, "Up until the day I heard the *Circle* album, I was a classical violinist. Forever then after, I called myself a fiddler. I spent two weeks learning 'Lonesome Fiddle Blues' and never turned back." Many people like Phil have been affected by it.

SPL: What is bluegrass music's appeal on the international level? I recall the Dirt Band toured Russia in 1977.

JM: Part of the appeal internationally of bluegrass I believe stems from the fact that, worldwide, all forms of music that are popular with masses of people, with "the people," not necessarily the highest part of the cultures, they all have rapid notes, rapidity of whatever you call them, eighth or sixteenth notes. Turkish music, Chinese, Irish *(John demonstrates, making the sound of rapidly playing notes)*. Bluegrass has a lot of that. So, that's one of its international appeals.

SPL: The *Circle* albums, as in bluegrass, demonstrate many family connections. Why do you think the ties that bind are so strong within bluegrass and traditional music?

JM: You have to ask the kids. I'm just pleased by it. I think … it reaches somewhere deeper in people than they can explain sometimes. I don't know why Ronnie and Robbie McCoury like to play with their dad, but they sure do.

SPL: Jeff, how do we reach out to the next generation to cultivate an appreciation for bluegrass music in them?

JH: I think it's been a continuing cycle since the music became popular when Bill Monroe, and then later Flatt and Scruggs, burst on the scene. I think there's always been a continuing generational turnover in these bands. Lots of guys cut their teeth on the music playing with Bill Monroe, and a lot of them later with Lester and Earl. There's also an expanding of the circle, so to speak, musically, too. I think there's just so much great stuff. Alison Krauss + Union Station, of course, who have been around for awhile now, are a great example of a younger band finding their own niche, as it were, in this kind of music. Then you have kids like Nickel Creek who are phenomenal, one of the best. They're so incredibly talented.

To me the future is really bright. . . . It's always great to do stuff that was written years ago, and it's also great to hear people use a bluegrass foundation for playing more modern music, too. So I don't think there's any danger in it being lost anywhere. I heard somebody say the other day that Chris Thile from Nickel Creek is doing for the mandolin what Tiger Woods is doing for golf clubs. That's a pretty good analogy. Your kids want to go out and get one. That's the kind of thing I think bluegrass and acoustic music in general has needed. You need to find somebody that captures the younger generation's imagination.

When I was a kid, there were people like Doc Watson that inspired me. As much as I tried slowing those records down and learning "Black Mountain Rag," I still can't play it, but it certainly inspired me to play. Period. He's such a great singer, such a great guy.

This music is really a treasure. It doesn't seem to be the kind of treasure that the people that are really great at it want to horde. It seems as if they want to share it, you know, pass it along. That's the beauty. One of the things I love about bluegrass festivals is that there's so much standing around, playing, sharing licks, and sharing songs. It's a beautiful thing.

SPL: How do you preserve the tradition of bluegrass while expanding on it to reach out to others?

JH: I think the tradition is the foundation. I know that, when I was a kid, the first folk music that I was exposed to were traditional songs like "Banks of the Ohio" or Woody Guthrie songs. Pete Seeger was a big inspiration for me, and he did a great job of passing the folk music torch and exposing people to music and songs that he had been playing for years and years. He is a great teacher and wonderful guiding light in folk music overall. I noticed that what happened with me as a kid, when I started listening to folk music, I was first exposed to the commercial stuff, like Peter, Paul and Mary and the Kingston Trio. But I heard songs in their repertoire that made me want to go back further and kind of get a history lesson on it. I think it's always great to know where it came from, if you really want to kind of create your own thing.

SPL: Look into the future and tell me who will be on the fiftieth anniversary version of the *Circle* album.

JH: *(Laughs heartily)* Well, assuming that we can still pick and sing by then, you know, it's really hard to say. Of course, there are our kids, between Jaime, my son, and John's boy, Jonathan, that were great on this new record that we just did. Now they're a good example. And Nickel Creek, of course, that'd be a natural progression. If we wait another twenty years, Alison Krauss will be the matriarch of bluegrass music. So, that gives you a pretty good idea.

I'm sure that there are tons of people that are out there who are waiting in the wings. This is all a natural cycle. One of the things I love about what we do is you don't have to stop playing just because you pass the fifty-year mark or the sixty-year mark, Earl Scruggs being a great example, Doc Watson being a great example. And just in music in general, Tony Bennett sings as well as he ever did right now. It can go on and on.

There's always got to be that next sort of layer. Every plant has to sprout some new growth. The forest needs new trees. It's a natural cycle for things to move on. But one of the things I love about this music is the love for its traditions and the people that have continued playing it through the years. I'm sure it'll be in great hands.

Interview conducted October 24, 2002, Count Basie Theatre, Red Bank, New Jersey.

8

The International Language of Bluegrass

Dateline: Mars, February 27, 2004. The wake-up song of the day for the Mars rover, Spirit, was Pete and Joan Wernick's Country Cooking version of "Big Rock in the Road," a hard-driving banjo song also found on Del McCoury's 1972 *High on a Mountain* album. The song was aptly selected to prepare Spirit to make its final approach to an imposing rock dubbed "Humphrey," which it was to cut into for study.[1]

Bluegrass might be homegrown in America, but its appeal extends across oceans—and planets. Aficionados turn up in such seemingly unlikely places as Australia, Israel, and China.

Today with bluegrass fans and musicians found on at least five continents, the Internet assists in bringing bluegrass enthusiasts in closer contact with each other. Since the mid-seventies, the international scene for bluegrass has mushroomed.

No one can say when bluegrass first crossed borders and captured attention from the Far East to the former Eastern bloc to Down Under. However, there are a number of defining activities that helped carry the high lonesome sound to non-English-speaking countries.

Bill Clifton, mentioned in chapter 4, moved to England in the early sixties and from there introduced bluegrass to a brand new audience, ripe and receptive to music whose English, Irish, and Scotch roots had sprung from beneath their feet but had skipped across an ocean and back again.

Clifton became the premier ambassador for bluegrass abroad. He produced a radio show on the BBC, a special program for Moscow Radio, and toured throughout Europe. Clifton's travels and work in the Peace Corps then took him to the Philippines, to New Zealand, and eventually back to

[1]See http://marsrovers.jpl.nasa.gov/mission/status_spiritAll.html#sol54.

the United States. Nevertheless, bluegrass remained in the minds and hearts of its newfound enthusiasts in these far-flung places.

Close on Clifton's well-traveled heels was the McLain Family Band of Berea, Kentucky. During its two decades with "Daddy" Raymond K. McLain at the helm, the McLain Family Band made fourteen trips abroad, bringing bluegrass and traditional music to sixty-two countries. Many of these tours were made under the auspices of the Department of State. As ambassadors of America's homegrown music, the McLains were the first bluegrass group to perform in many foreign lands. Among the countless places they traveled, armed with fiddles, banjos, and mandolins, were Africa, Burma, Nepal, Romania, and Italy.

The Nashville Bluegrass Band made history when it became the first bluegrass group to perform in The People's Republic of China. Audiences in such countries as Brazil, Israel, and Egypt have enjoyed a taste of this ensemble's unmatched harmony singing. Many other artists, including Bill Monroe and the Blue Grass Boys, J.D. Crowe and the New South, and Del McCoury have carried bluegrass around the globe.

Starting in the sixties, Japan was among the earliest to open its doors to bluegrass. Flatt and Scruggs was the first American bluegrass band to perform there in 1968, followed by Ralph Stanley, the Country Gentlemen, and Bill Monroe—and that was just the initial six years of concerts produced in Japan. It has been nonstop since that time.

Throughout the years, the American Forces Network (AFN) has been instrumental in carrying a number of country music programs to military personnel stationed abroad. Much of what was heard in the early days was bluegrass and its predecessor forms.

The *Louisiana Hayride* was one such popular program. During World War II, condensed *Grand Ole Opry* programs were broadcast, taken from the Prince Albert NBC Network for the Armed Forces. A posting on a Web page maintained by the Armed Forces Radio and Television Service mentioned that, in the mid-fifties, out of Frankfurt, Germany, soldiers could tune in to such shows as *Hillbilly Gasthaus* or Tommy Cash's *Stickbuddy Jamboree.*[2]

In 1945, when World War II ended, the U.S. military built a radio station in Japan, WVTR, carrying what was then called the Far East Network (FEN) and now AFN. Among the entertainment that was broadcast was a hillbilly music program called *Honshu Hayride.* Jazz, Hawaiian, and country-and-western were the most popular genres of the day, but eventually a bluegrasslike band, the East Mountain Boys, emerged around 1956.

However, it was a hundred years before that, March 27, 1854, that banjo debuted in Japan. Brought there by Commodore Perry, four days ahead of the signing of the Japan–U.S. Treaty of Peace and Amity, the Japanese Olio Minstrels entertained for the party with banjo, fiddle, and other instruments.

[2]See http://www.afrts.osd.mil/heritage/page.asp?pg=archive_email1.

It was the first American music played in Japan. Among the songs they shared were "Angelina Baker," "Old Tar River," and "Get Up in de Morning."

Saburo "Watanabe" Inoue, who today remains the prime mover of all things bluegrass in Japan, recalls that he started to play around 1962 or 1963 while in junior high school. There was a folk music club, the first in Japan, called Lost City in downtown Kobe where the Backwood Mountain Boys would play each weekend. When they disbanded in 1967, a new group, Blue-grass 45, soon merged with some of its members and others, including Saburo and his brother, Toshio, both of whom had been involved with the folk club.

Bluegrass 45 made history when it came to the United States in 1971. It was a first for Japanese bluegrass, and the band started at the top, so to speak, playing Bill Monroe's Bean Blossom Festival before embarking on a three-month tour of the United States and Canada. On that tour, the band also played on the *Opry* at the Ryman Auditorium in Nashville. By the next year, however, when the members returned for their second stateside tour, Inoue had left the band to establish, with assistance from Toshio, B.O.M. (Bluegrass and Old-Time Music) Service Ltd. A multifaceted agency, B.O.M. incorpo-rates festival promotion, a record label, and mail order for bluegrass record-ings and materials. In addition, the company publishes *Moonshiner*, a bluegrass magazine begun in 1983. Its predecessor was *June Apple*, no longer published.

The first large-scale festival in Japan was held in 1972, the Takarazuka Bluegrass Festival, which Inoue continues to oversee. Two smaller events occurred before that, a jamboree hosted by the Lost City coffeehouse and a two-day event in 1971 in Karuizawa, but it lacked the structure of a for-mal festival atmosphere.

While Inoue insists that bluegrass is "not that popular" in Japan, it is all relative. He modestly says that there are only around three hundred active bluegrass bands and twenty-five annual bluegrass festivals. He related that there are "no more than five thousand die-hard bluegrass fans." Moreover, while it is true, just as in the United States, that those figures make it diffi-cult to make a living working only in bluegrass, it certainly says volumes about bluegrass and its international appeal. Inoue's company has just five employees, yet it handles all of the previously mentioned activities.

Asked why Japanese love bluegrass so much in spite of little comprehen-sion of the lyrics, Inoue replied that "In the music, you only need to un-derstand the feeling of the notes, not the meaning of the lyrics. You need a deep ear and heart to understand this music. Once you understand this art form or you try to play it, you'll understand how this music has depth.

"I think only two musics can be world music from the U.S.," he went on. "It's jazz and bluegrass . . . and it's no longer an American music . . . sorry about that!" he stated enthusiastically.

Inoue continued to make one more interesting, heartfelt point. "Now you'll ask, what's the difference between rock, folk, or country and jazz and bluegrass? Well, you can play rock, folk, or country even if you don't know Elvis, Pete, or Hank, because it's a culture and feelings. However, you can't play jazz or bluegrass if you don't know Louis or Bill, because it's a form and it takes a special ear for it."

It is difficult to ascertain the definitive route bluegrass took to reach the ears of many it might not otherwise have reached. Banjos and fiddles have made their way to various outposts where American military personnel are stationed, for example. Radio has certainly played a large role, as have re-cords— 78s, LPs, 45 rpm singles—and, more recently, CDs, as they made their way into stores in Germany, Italy, the Philippines. Here is another in-teresting account of how bluegrass bypassed Customs, holding only the in-ternational language of the music itself as its passport.

During the late seventies in Greece, "cowboy" music (i.e., bluegrass and old-time) was used as filler for an hour preceding Sunday soccer ball games, a time slot difficult to sell to advertisers because it is the customary "siesta" hour there—nobody would be listening; they would be resting postlunch, pregame. This was mainstream commercial radio, one of the two largest sta-tions with broad coverage across the country. The theory is the music prob-ably filtered into the station's archives from a long-forgotten cultural exchange program.

From Genoa, Italy, Beppe Gambetta often relates his early introduction to bluegrass. Already enamored with guitar as a youngster, he stumbled across a record with Doc Watson playing "Black Mountain Rag." That caught his attention immediately, as did a second cut featuring Lester Flatt and Earl Scruggs. From then on, Gambetta lived and breathed bluegrass. He went on to cofound in 1977 the Italian bluegrass group Red Wine. To-day, Gambetta is recognized around the world as one of the top flatpickers but no longer the only Italian flatpicker.

Red Wine has continued without Gambetta since 1988. Just as with many American bluegrass groups, the members did not give up their day jobs to pursue music yet are a highly polished, professional act. Mandolinist Martino Coppo, long-time member and an attorney in his "other life," spoke about bluegrass and its universal appeal during an interview on August 31, 2003, in New Jersey where Red Wine was making a festival appearance.

SPL: Why do you think fans in Italy have embraced American bluegrass?

MC: The harmony singing, power of the playing, the drive that comes from not just the banjo but also the whole band working together. The acoustic aspect is very natural, too. The sound, soul, the intensity of everything, even pauses are somehow intense in real bluegrass, which is sometimes difficult to reproduce on record. It can sound colder than it is. The atmosphere and the impact at a festival is a lot different than on record. Ask a European blue-grass fan and he will cite the virtuosity and technique. But voices like Dan

Tyminski, just guitar and voice, it grabs your heart and nails you down to the bluegrass sound.

SPL: What was your introduction to bluegrass?

MC: A New Grass Revival album was the first bluegrass-sounding band that I heard. I fell in love with it almost immediately. Silvio [Ferretti, banjo] came out of the folk tradition, Pete Seeger, Mike Seeger, Emmylou [Harris], Doc Watson. After we met, I learned the differences between the traditional and the more progressive, and the different crowds in the U.S. and in Italy.

SPL: Red Wine absolutely nails the American sound. Who did you listen to that you have learned from?

MC: Everyone!

SPL: What would you like to tell newcomers to bluegrass?

MC: Go to a good bluegrass festival first, where you really can feel the music. Invest in a weekend there; you'll be a newborn fan. You know, it's the people that make bluegrass so special, make it just wonderful.

At first glance, it might seem odd to think that an American-born genre could or would be so popular in countries beyond the United States. But when one examines the indigenous musical instruments as well as the traditional folk musics themselves of various foreign folk cultures, it is not such a stretch to see why the ears of non-Americans perk up to the sounds of bluegrass.

From the lively, frenzied fiddling to the sorrowful, introspective tunes, many similarities can be heard throughout the world's various, yet ultimately related, folk forms. In the realm of today's popular crossover artists and others who collaborate on unusual pairings of music, these lines blur even further with such cultural infusions. Stringed instruments used in any number of different countries or cultures are often essentially the same instrument, only the name has changed. An example is the Appalachian dulcimer described in chapter 5. Fiddles (or violins) come in a variety of sizes, number of strings, and tunings around the world. Greece's bouzouki is quite similar to mandolin, itself originally an Italian instrument.

The hammered dulcimer, while not a "bluegrass" instrument, per se, is found in many other countries as well as in the States. In Switzerland, for example, it is known as the *hackbrett*, and it is often played accompanied by the violin, bowed bass fiddle, and accordion. Listen to the traditional folk music of the canton of Appenzell, whose colorful costumes and dangling silver-spoon earrings worn by men and boys complete the picture. The strains and tempo could just as easily fit into a bluegrass jam session.

For Ola Berge, a talent agent from Oslo, Norway, it was, in part, the differences between bluegrass and traditional Norwegian folk music that attracted him to the sound. Already familiar with Celtic music and its many facets, he shared some thoughts while in Nashville to attend the annual Folk Alliance conference in February 2003.

> I was a fan of Celtic, Irish, and American country music. When I first heard bluegrass, I just instantly knew that was the American version of the Celtic traditional folk music. I was amazed by the brilliant technique, the skillful musicians playing in a virtuoso way. That really blew my mind. It's very impressive.
>
> When I'm presenting the Norwegian music, it's not really virtuoso music. It doesn't go fast, and that's sort of a shame, because it takes longer to get people into it. Bluegrass has the speed and energy.
>
> There is not too much similarity in bluegrass to Norwegian music. Except in the singing, the blue notes, the way to make things sound sad or bluesy. That's also the same with a lot of American country music, like Hank Williams. There are lots of similarities in singing.
>
> I prefer traditional bluegrass, the old recordings. People were making music in a different way fifty and one hundred years ago. They were thinking in another manner.

And who is Berge's favorite bluegrass musician? "Bill Monroe and his fellow musicians," he replied, but added quickly, "and close to bluegrass without being bluegrass is Hank Williams."

Norway has approximately ten bluegrass bands and also hosts an annual event each July, the Risor Bluegrass Festival. Next door in Sweden, there are about ten to twenty active bands, among them the Downhill Bluegrass Band and Mountain Folks. The largest bluegrass festival there is in Gränna and has been around for more than twenty-five years. Longtime president of the American Folk Music Association there is Robert Ahl, who arranged the tour that resulted in the classic album *Live in Sweden* with the White Brothers, among Clarence's final recordings before his death in 1973.

One of the hottest hotbeds for bluegrass is the Czech Republic along with its neighbor and former "partner," Slovakia. This is not surprising if you think back to chapter 5 and the discussion about the dobro and its inventor. Not only do these two countries boast numerous top-notch bluegrass and newgrass bands, they have many successful annual festivals, including the Dobro Fest in Trnava, Slovakia, as well as luthiers of fine bluegrass instruments. Fragment and Druhá Tráva are two of the most successful groups who tour internationally.

France, Germany, the Netherlands, Brazil, Australia, Great Britain, and Switzerland are just a few more countries where you can find great bluegrass music on a regular basis. All have very active and involved bluegrass scenes, many with local membership associations, annual festivals, and numerous concerts by local as well as traveling American bands.

Since 1980, Groundspeed, with Swiss and German roots, has been a leading multinational band. Interestingly, the members rely on early bluegrass and its raw, old-time roots, performing such songs as "When the Roses Bloom in Dixieland," complete with close "brother" harmonies. Bulgaria boasts Lilly of the West, its one and only bluegrass group. The Krüger Brothers are a breakthrough Swiss band that has been quite popular for many years with American audiences as well as European. It has been so successful, that its members have moved to North Carolina to continue their career. And Germany's Fox Tower Bluegrass Band has been a bedrock for more than two decades.

From Russia, there have been two groups that have captured much attention in the United States. In the late eighties and early nineties, a group called Kukuruza ("corn" in Russian) took American audiences by storm with distinctive virtuosity and rousing vocals. More recently, Bering Strait arrived in America, all of its members giving up their lives in Russia to follow bluegrass. Although they have moved into music that is more country than bluegrass, they continue to attract attention for their talent and success story. They have been featured in the *New York Times*, and a documentary, *The Ballad of Bering Strait*, was made about these unusual, classically trained musicians now living in Nashville.

Spain has a small but enthusiastic bluegrass community, numbering around one hundred and primarily centered in Barcelona, Madrid, and Bilbao. Because of the difficulties of sustaining an exclusively bluegrass scene, the fewer than a dozen active groups also play other related musics, such as Celtic or country. They have recently attempted to establish an annual event each June in Barcelona.

Based in that city, Heribert Ródenas and Maria Ricart play banjo and mandolin, respectively, and formed a group, Bandana, in 1985. After only a couple of very active years, the band is more of a "garage" band these days, yet Ródenas and Ricart keep abreast of the music. They cite several French bluegrass and acoustic music festivals as integral to their interest and continued participation in bluegrass.

Ricart explained that the couple met at a folk festival and that "Heri first liked the sound of the banjo; I was fascinated by the mandolin." Heri originally heard many records of such artists as Flatt and Scruggs, Bill Keith, and the Kentucky Colonels.

Continuing, Ricart said, "We agree that we liked [bluegrass] because it's acoustic. For us it was a fresh sound, participative. We also liked the vocal harmonies and the combination with instrumental solos."

North of the U.S. border, the wide spaces of Canada maintain several organizations along with numerous festivals. A national magazine, *Bluegrass Canada*, served fans for many years but is no longer publishing. As this book was going to press, a new bimonthly publication was announced. *Bluegrass North* was scheduled to debut in late 2004. In the meantime, regional newsletters cover news and events of the many bands and jams.

South of the border, all the way south, in São Paolo, Brazil, you will find an energetic, thriving bluegrass community. There, a local bluegrass association brings together members for concerts, jam sessions, and more, while fostering cultural exchange with the local folk music, such as *choro*.

In 1989, Bob Wolff, a mandolin-picking bluegrass fan, put forth an idea intended to attract more attention to bluegrass in order to cultivate its viability as a music genre. With the help of fans around the globe, he kicked off the very first "Celebrate May! Worldwide Bluegrass Music Month."

Each year during the month of May, a diverse array of activities occurs in the United States, in Europe, Japan, Australia, Canada, and virtually everywhere bluegrass has a presence. These events range from "pick-ins" at shopping malls and parks to concerts, festivals, and special get-togethers. Because of the concentration of activities within only a month's time, media attention is attracted and many of these annual projects attract new fans each year. Such exposure is meant to increase popularity for the music, thereby creating better and more performance opportunities for bluegrass musicians.

Wolff put the idea out specifically for the development of larger audiences for bluegrass. It is a unique concept in that it is not sponsored by any one umbrella organization or company. Wolff is not in charge of it, the "concept," nor is anyone else. It is simply an idea carried by the music itself around the world via proactive enthusiasts who, each year, go out of their way to see that May is extra-filled with bluegrass activities in local communities. Whether it is a fiddle workshop in Wichita, Kansas; a bluegrass barbecue outside of London, England; a jam session in a local high school in Chicago; or a full-scale bluegrass festival in Australia, fans are encouraged to share the music with others, especially bluegrass newcomers.

The Society for the Preservation of Bluegrass Music of America (SPBGMA) was formed in 1975 "to preserve the traditional spirit and art form of bluegrass music." Several festivals are sponsored each year in various locations, mostly in the Midwest region of the United States. Its crowning event is a large-scale February festival, band competition, and awards presentation. Performers and fans travel to Nashville from across the country and from overseas to attend and participate.

In 1985, a trade organization was established, the International Bluegrass Music Association (IBMA). Its stated mission is "Working together for high standards of professionalism, a greater appreciation for our music, and the success of the worldwide bluegrass community."

Each fall, IBMA hosts the World of Bluegrass, where artists, agents, event promoters, journalists, broadcasters, record label personnel, and countless other professionals working in bluegrass, along with fans, many of whom volunteer their energies hosting radio shows and running local associations, all have the opportunity to interact. Networking, seminars, exhibits, and artist showcases comprise a professionally oriented trade show.

The trade show culminates in the International Bluegrass Music Awards, as elaborately produced as similar presentations for country music, for example. Heard throughout the world, the program is the largest annual media event designed to promote bluegrass music and has been recognized in such publications as *USA Today.*

A weekend Fan Fest, open to the general public, with stage presentations, workshops, and vendors, wraps up the World of Bluegrass week. Originally held in Kentucky, the event moves to Nashville in the fall of 2005.

In 1998, IBMA assisted the European bluegrass community in establishing its own annual World of Bluegrass event on the Continent. Other festivals have followed suit as bluegrass organizations continue to emerge in various countries across Europe. As of 2004, the IBMA membership hovered around 2,500 worldwide, with all fifty states and thirty countries represented.

9

Up Close: Concerts, Festivals, and Parking Lot Pickin'

As a newcomer to bluegrass, you will, of course, want to hear bluegrass up close and personal, take in a concert or two, join a picking session to test those fresh hot licks you've been practicing, or, best of all, pack up your gear and head out to your first bluegrass festival.

You have not experienced bluegrass fully until, and unless, you have attended a bluegrass festival. Tradition is that it's got to be hot and/or rainy and that you get little, if any, sleep. The air is thick with humidity, so heavy that water beads off you within five minutes of stepping out of your air-conditioned car onto the festival site. You are greeted by snippets of sparkling banjo rolls echoing around you from all directions and harmony vocals, unusually high pitched, hanging above soulful fiddle breaks—nothing like any fiddle you've heard the local symphony play.

Everyone around you seems oblivious to the heat and the cacophonous groups of parking lot pickers and singers scattered everywhere, each in unintended competition with the other. Some are gathered under dining canopies; others lean against cars. Omigosh, there's a group picking behind the port-a-johns; must have something to do with natural acoustics.

A sea of lawn chairs separates you from the stage, where an ensemble of spiffy-looking musicians in white cowboy hats is playing in earnest. The musicians don't seem to notice the sweat droplets running down their faces and splash-painting their instruments. Looking across the field, a patchwork quilt of tents, campers, RVs, and dining flies covers the terrain, like a still-life cross between Remington and Rockwell. Conversations pick up where they left off at the last festival, last weekend's or last year's. How high did you set the action on that new guitar? What kind of strings are you using? Do you know the words to . . . ? Your kid picks like Earl and he's HOW old?

You claim your spot and park yourself for the next several hours on a hill where you can take in every set on stage and where, if you're lucky, a dead twig from a pitiful parched tree long-gone provides at least a ray of shade. Or maybe you got there early enough to grab your two-foot-square parcel of ground right up front, you know, rather close to those megaspeakers that will render you all but blissfully deaf by the end of the weekend.

Just beyond the stage, there's a large pavilion containing a colorful panoply of vendors. They are selling everything from souvenir festival T-shirts and hats to handmade jewelry and custom-built guitars. Alongside is the performer "meet and greet" area toward which a hundred fans sprint as the final notes sound on stage, each wanting to be first in line to "shake and howdy" with their favorite musician and buy a CD.

You might wake up to a lone fiddle playing—correction, you are awakened by your neighbor two tents over. He is sawing out an exceptionally out-of-tune rendition of "The Kentucky Waltz" in anticipation of joining a jam session a bit later. He's been playing fiddle only about three months, so he thought he'd get in a little practice while there's downtime on stage; it's 7:30 a.m. You only just got to sleep about three hours earlier—rocked by the lullaby of banjos still ringing across the field and through the campsite in those darkest hours before dawn.

The inviting smell of eggs frying somewhere nearby begins to permeate your senses. So you crawl out of your hot and dusty pop-up (or damp and muggy, if it teemed all night) and you head for the portable showers—if this festival happens to boast on-site water—where, naturally, that not-yet-warmed-by-the-sun water opens your eyes quicker than the fastest lick.

Ah, but there's music all around. It's just going on 10 a.m. Someone is tuning a mandolin over by the concession area that is just beginning to bustle with activity. You spot a kid wearing and playing a guitar bigger than he is, but a small crowd has gathered in awe of what appears to be a twelve-year-old wunderkind. If it's Sunday morning, you can already discern the harmonized notes of rousing gospel coming from the stage area.

There's a tired but satisfied grin waking up on your face as you think back to the night before. You've got the digital picture to prove how, after their sets, you actually got to meet Rhonda Vincent and Del McCoury.

Long about eight, nine o'clock that night, after you've had far more hot dogs and ice cream cones than you care to admit, and just when you thought you couldn't stand the heat any longer, the skies open up. Glued to the evening's headliner, few people leave their chairs in spite of the downpour. Rain ponchos and umbrellas quickly appear, and the show continues against the noisy backdrop of a summer's passing rainstorm.

The air clears, the stickiness seems to lift, and it gets just a couple of degrees cooler as four white cowboy hats all gather around one microphone on stage. All is dead quiet as they harmonize a cappella, ending the evening with a standing ovation. Stars appear in the night sky as you wander off to listen in or sit in on as many picking parties as you can take in before fatigue drags you back to your campsite. No one has missed a beat, not the musicians, not the fans, not the parking lot pickers, not even the crickets chirping in tune that have found safe haven in your tent.

THE PEOPLES' MUSIC

Hearing bluegrass, even an entire live performance, on CD cannot replace hearing it live, up close and personal. To see the interaction of the musicians, the earnest look on their faces as they strive to play faster, with greater precision, challenging each other's licks and runs, sweat rolling down their brows, it just does something to you that is difficult to put into words.

The camaraderie that develops at festivals, concerts, and other get-togethers is an important aspect of bluegrass music. Bluegrass is very much a community of like-minded individuals, a "family." Musicians are accessible, usually not held off at arm's length from fans by security fencing. They are among the most approachable and "non-starlike" performers around, more so than those in most any other genre of music. They mingle freely, gladly giving autographs, grins, and good advice about picking technique.

Bluegrass festivals are a relatively recent phenomenon. While multiple-day bluegrass festivals were first established in the mid-sixties, festivals themselves go back much further.

As discussed in chapter 5, fiddle contests date to Colonial times. Early large-scale fiddlers' conventions, primarily found in the South, became part model for the first folk festivals in the 1920s, which originated in the South. These departed from the fiddlers' convention style in that they were established with the intent of attracting others besides musicians to attend, in other words, the general public. Bluegrass festivals are a contemporary form of original folk festivals. Modern-day folk festivals differ as well, often comprising a wide variety of genres and typically leaning toward "new" folk styles, world music, and newgrass or other innovative blends.

Today's bluegrass festivals come in all sizes and flavors, from weekend-long to weeklong events held on campgrounds and farms to downtown one-day street fairs. There are specially themed bluegrass cruises or home-style town activities, such as an "Apple Butter Stirrin'" celebration that might feature bluegrass in its entertainment. A handful of festivals are held in large luxury hotels, hosting pickers in carpeted lounges and ballrooms.

Bluegrass-exclusive festivals alone easily tally a thousand each year in the United States and several foreign countries; to find double that would not be surprising. Add all the folk festivals, "eclectic acoustic" festivals, and unusual events that include some bluegrass, and the possibilities are infinite. There is no way to know the exact number.

Furthermore, you don't have to wait for spring or summer to enjoy a bluegrass or newgrass festival. Year-round, there is something for everyone. For example, end and start your year with Georgia's Jekyll Island New Year's Bluegrass Festival, a fairly traditional bluegrass and gospel event. In February,

travel on to Wintergrass in the state of Washington; plush hotel accommodations await you. Ditto on the hotel in Nashville, where you can catch the
annual SPBGMA Awards and National Convention. Take the kids on an early
spring break in March to Florida's Disney resort, and a stone's throw away
you can attend the Kissimmee Bluegrass Festival.

Spring is the more "official" start of festival season when your choices
begin to expand. In April in Texas, you can head over to the Old Settlers'
Bluegrass Festival in Austin. At the end of April and beginning of May with
"Celebrate May! Worldwide Bluegrass Music Month" in view, get on track
with the Lewis Family's Annual Homecoming and Bluegrass Festival in
Lincolnton, Georgia, or grab your hiking shoes for MerleFest in North Carolina. MerleFest spans a large, hilly college campus and features a dozen stages
of eclectic acoustic music choices.

May also offers the spring Gettysburg (Pennsylvania) Bluegrass Festival
as well as the Strawberry Spring Music Festival, located adjacent to Yosemite
Park in California. Or why not fly across the Atlantic for the European World
of Bluegrass Festival in the Netherlands?

June busts out all over. Hang out in California for the Grass Valley Father's
Day Bluegrass Festival, enjoy bluegrass in the Bluegrass State at the Festival
of the Bluegrass in Lexington, or pick among the trees at the Wind Gap
(Pennsylvania) Bluegrass Festival. Of course, you might instead opt for the
Bill Monroe Memorial Bean Blossom Bluegrass Festival in Indiana where you
have weekend through weekend activities, one of the longest among bluegrass events.

July is hot no matter where you choose to go for your mid-summer dose
of bluegrass. RockyGrass in Colorado offers splendid vistas in addition to
superpicker music. The East Coast choices include Grey Fox Bluegrass Festival in upstate New York or the unusual "O*A*T*S" (*Out Among The
Stars*) Bluegrass Festival in Benton, Pennsylvania, a concept festival begun
by a bunch of die-hard fans and pickers, the Grillbillies. And, yes, as the name
implies, there's plenty of food a-cookin', too.

Don't wind down yet; August has lots in store. Camp out in Japan at the
Takarazuka Bluegrass Festival north of Kobe, and when you wake up, you
will swear you're in Tennessee. The Minnesota Bluegrass and Old-Time
Music Festival provides still another panorama, while down in Hugo, Texas,
Grant's Bluegrass Festival continues under the same management since its
start in 1969. A fun, full-day affair is Bill Knowlton's Bluegrass Ramble Pic-
nic; Knowlton is host to one of America's longest running bluegrass radio
programs, *Bluegrass Ramble*, aired out of central New York State.

Labor Day weekend heading into September offers not-quite-the-last-
hurrah of festival season. The Delaware Valley Bluegrass Festival has three
days of music at the Salem County Fairgrounds in Woodstown, New Jersey,
while up in Maine, the Thomas Point Beach Bluegrass Festival competes.
September keeps the music going with Poppy Mountain Bluegrass Festival

in Kentucky, or how about the Bluegrass and Chili Festival, formerly held annually in Tulsa, now relocated to Claremore, Oklahoma?

The granddaddy of flatpicking festivals, without a doubt, is smack dab in the middle of the United States. Winfield, Kansas, is home to the Walnut Valley Festival, where festival-goers show up a week in advance to claim their campsites, renew friendships, and jam till dawn each day. Fall is greeted by the Oklahoma International Bluegrass Festival in Guthrie as well as by IBMA's Bluegrass Fan Fest, held in Kentucky through 2004 and moving to Nashville in 2005.

November might bring cold weather to some, but Myrtle Beach is the place to escape to for the South Carolina State Bluegrass Festival. Then it's time to start packing for Jekyll Island once again in December.

STARS AND "ORDINARY FOLK"

During the first couple of decades of bluegrass festivals, more clearly delineated distinctions could be found between the very traditional camps and the more progressively styled events. For example, electric bass, or any electric instrument or drums, was prohibited at most festivals, a practice still found at some today.

In part due to a more receptive, younger audience and recently attributed to insightful marketing moves, a greater number of bluegrass festivals are embracing a diversified selection of traditional and progressive bluegrass acts for their stages. With literally hundreds of events, large and small, to choose from, there is a lot to be said for both, and one is not necessarily a "better" festival than the other based on style alone. A solid talent lineup, good site facilities, and, most of all, a well-managed festival make for a wonderful festival experience for the newcomer or the experienced festival-goer.

It is not unusual to find your favorite star, dressed in "disguise" in jeans and a ball cap, out jamming until all hours with "ordinary folk" long after the stage has shut down for the night. Bluegrass fans are probably among the most devoted to their music over any other form around, and bluegrass artists are among the most attentive, cognizant, and respectful of their fans.

Bluegrass musicians will go to great lengths to perform for you. It is not at all unusual for bands to drive very long distances between gigs. One by one at the conclusion of a performance or festival, band buses pull out heading to the next gig. Often these drives will take them across several states overnight to arrive an hour before show time the next day. Many groups take shifts driving through the night; others hire drivers.

Before they pull out and move on, you can be sure they have spent as much time as it takes to talk to all their waiting fans, signing autographs at the CD sales tables and posing for endless photographs. Often this ritual goes on for an hour or two after the last note has been sung, well into a long night ahead. Yet you will see these seemingly tireless performers patiently—

and with a smile on their faces—talk to their fans right up to the last one waiting. Bluegrass musicians care.

Let me interject—bring cash, lots of it, or a checkbook. Although some are able to accept credit cards, most artists do not. You will want to buy CDs and other products after you hear and see the bands. And you will want to purchase more than you might think you would. Buying directly from a performer at a festival or a concert has three advantages: instant gratification (pop it in your vehicle's CD changer on the long drive home); you can get it autographed; and the entire cost of the CD goes directly into the artist's pocket.

Two other activities that occur at festivals, in addition to stage performances, are workshops and jam sessions. Workshops are forums for learning more about playing technique for a specific instrument, harmony singing, songwriting, clog dancing, or perhaps a discussion about the history of bluegrass. Workshops vary widely. More about festival workshops will be discussed in the next chapter. Many festivals feature music activities geared to youth, while some sport play areas for kids to let energies loose.

Parking lot pickin' is a tradition as solid as tailgate picnicking before football games. Age is no barrier, young or old, nor is level of ability. On key or off, parking lot picking is all about the love of the music and contributing what you will in terms of your licks, your voice, or just hang out and enjoy.

These jam sessions are found at just about every turn. Parking lot picking, as you might well imagine, is just that, people jamming out among the parked cars and campers. The campgrounds often turn into numerous ministages. At larger festivals, there could be, literally, dozens of separate jams going on simultaneously.

CONNECTING WITH THE LOCAL SCENE

The two major bluegrass organizations mentioned in the previous chapter, the International Bluegrass Music Association (IBMA) and the Society for the Preservation of Bluegrass Music of America (SPBGMA), are excellent sources for connecting both locally and on a grander scale. Both have resources to draw on that can facilitate your pursuit of bluegrass. They each have directories available, sponsor a variety of events and activities, and can put you in further contact with bluegrass folks in your area.

To get connected with the bluegrass "action" and find out who's playing where, the best route is through your local bluegrass or folk music club or organization. There are hundreds around the country as well as overseas. Networking with other bluegrass aficionados will give you additional invaluable insight into the music and its performers. Getting recommendations about concerts, recordings, instructors, or makes of instruments is always helpful coming from others who might know more than you do. Bluegrass enthusiasts love to share their music.

Start with the resources suggested in Where to from Here; they will lead to more specific ones for your vicinity. Most local bluegrass associations exist solely to foster the music, that is, they sponsor a range of activities from informal weekly or monthly jam sessions to regular concerts in small venues with "name" acts or local bands. Town parks often host free outdoor summer concerts. Furthermore, most organizations either publish a newsletter or calendar of events or post the same information on an Internet site. Membership fees to support your local clubs are typically nominal and well worth the small investment. Newspaper weekend guides are an additional source for concerts, as are libraries and community bulletin boards. Some of the best local talent is stumbled upon this way.

Radio is a major source for bluegrass, whether on traditional radio, the Internet, or satellite. The majority of bluegrass-exclusive programming is typically—although not exclusively—found on noncommercial stations, that is, public radio or college-owned stations. Bluegrass associations as well as listings located on various Internet sites or in publications will lead you to bluegrass broadcast programming; several starting points can be found at the back of this book.

Jot down names of groups and songs that catch your attention. Some radio show hosts post their playlists online, which is extremely useful in seeking out recordings to buy from artists you've heard and liked. The greater diversity of styles that you expose yourself to while discovering bluegrass, the more you will enjoy. Each has its own special qualities.

Square or contra dancing is another activity hosted more typically by local folk organizations and less commonly by bluegrass associations but, nonetheless, relates to the music. Some organizations offer clogging workshops; 4-H clubs are a great source for children's teams. While the bluegrass "circle" is often "bluegrass only," you will find that local folk scenes typically serve as umbrella organizations to the overall "folk and bluegrass" community in your area. Be sure to look for both in checking out your possibilities.

A final key point to remember about seeing live bluegrass is how family-friendly bluegrass concerts and festivals are. Many festivals offer at least some, if not a full range of, children-specific activities, including age-appropriate performers, performances, and workshops. Teenage mandolin or fiddle champions are a great inspiration to other children their age and younger who are just starting out.

A popular concept, aimed at younger children, is instrument making from rudimentary materials, ending in a kids' "grand jam" led by real instruments. There are numerous books and Internet sites that offer construction guidelines for simple and inexpensive homemade instruments, among them washtub bass (from coffee cans and string), banjo or guitar (cigar or shoe box and string), or harmonica (comb and tissue paper).

Bluegrass provides an extra special cultural infusion to a child's music appreciation because it is homegrown American music. I have already mentioned many musicians who came from a bluegrass or early country music tradition within their families or who continue to keep it in the family. In "Pick It Up, Pass It On!" I will provide a brief overview of some of the instructional and educational opportunities for learning how to play, for adults as well as children.

During a weekend festival in 2003, I had occasion while ordering from the sno-cone stand to chat with its young concessionaire, a bluegrass fan. Actually, ten-year-old Taylor is the owner's daughter and was scooping like a pro as I stepped up. She was also obviously really enjoying the music, craning her neck to peer out at the stage area, all the while taking and filling orders. I asked her how she got into bluegrass and why she likes it. She explained that her folks listen to it and that she does too, in addition to country, pop, and rock. "It's just really good!" she explained. Taylor went on to "diss" loud rap and cursing in music, saying how bluegrass is "calming." Who is her favorite bluegrass performer? Without hesitation, "Ralph Stanley," she replied, beaming.

Age is simply not a barrier in bluegrass. It truly is a family-friendly music, enjoyed and played by a wide spectrum of ages. Many groups are multi-generational, while attendees make festival weekends a family affair. Whereas in some musical arenas it is discouraged to bring along the kids, here it is encouraged. Fiddlers as young as five or six enter competitions, and senior pickers abound. The next two chapters will take a peek at a few promising young talents.

For seniors, the example has been set by the founding fathers themselves. "Father of Bluegrass" Bill Monroe performed into his eighties, while Earl Scruggs and Doc Watson have recently entered theirs. Wilma Lee Cooper had just celebrated her eightieth birthday when forced to retire. Ralph Stanley, Jesse McReynolds, and Jimmy Martin all are in their seventies and active. Lewis Family patriarch, "Pop" Lewis, continued to tour and perform past his mid-nineties mark. Musician or fan, you don't retire from bluegrass.

10

Pick It Up, Pass It On!

Bluegrass! Pick it up!

A double entendre slogan developed to entice folks to listen to bluegrass, its intent was also aimed at musicians or musicians-to-be. While many simply prefer to sit back in their chairs and listen to the music at bluegrass festivals or concerts, there is a whole other side of bluegrass life when it comes to pickin'.

Bluegrass is a conducive, natural environment for participation. A key element of the community or family of bluegrass is the extraordinary number of fans who are also pickers, be they amateur, semipro/part-time, closet pickers, or even "air banjo" pickers. When compared with the general population surveyed by Simmons Research, bluegrass consumers were found to be more than twice as likely to play an instrument.

Now that you have, hopefully, been thoroughly bitten by the bluegrass bug, perhaps you want to learn to pick banjo like Earl or flatpick guitar as smartly as Doc. Maybe you want to show off how fast you can fiddle "Orange Blossom Special" for your sweetheart. Perhaps you have children already musically inclined whose horizons you would like to broaden with fun and wholesome bluegrass. Or now that you have taken that early retirement, you'd like to take all those lessons you had as a kid and turn your classical violin playing into bluegrass fiddling.

How or where does one start one's own journey to picker's paradise? And what opportunities are out there for you as well as for your children to learn?

The "Where to from Here" section lists a large number of resources for instructional methods and educational opportunities. A great place to start is your local bluegrass association or music store. They are likely to have several referrals of area teachers for specific instruments. Word-of-mouth recommendations are always a great path to pursue.

A handful of bluegrass "star" pickers manage to make time for individualized lessons in their hometowns. However, since most travel regularly, "in home" private lessons are provided by most "masters" in a different hands-on manner, that is, instructional videos, DVDs, and books. Literally something for everyone, there are hundreds of alternatives offered by many well-established companies whose instructors read like a who's who. From beginners who do not even know which end of an instrument to pick to those who want to jazz up their chops, the choices are endless.

One does not have to read music either. A method known as tablature is one of the easiest learning tools. A substitute for musical notation, tablature uses numbers or letters to denote which strings, frets, or keys are to be played. Varying playing levels are offered, including beginner, intermediate, and advanced. A diversity of styles, techniques, and specialties is also available. Among these are contest fiddling, basic flatpicking, favorite guitar solos, and cross-picking mandolin. Still others are "kid-friendly" lessons directed at children, some actually taught by teenagers and conveyed in a manner readily appreciated by the younger set.

Get recommendations from friends. If possible, chat with the musician whose instructional materials you are considering. Remember to take into account your playing level and abilities, your patience and time, and specifically what you are looking to learn. Are you looking for the basics, or are you looking for a novel technique to expand your skills? Are you looking to hone your hot licks?

If you have the opportunity to preview audio-video materials, take note of your comfort level with how the instructor presents the information, in addition to how well cameras capture up close the movements of both hands.

HANDS-ON WORKSHOPS

Popular at many festivals is the hands-on workshop setting. These vary, not only in subject matter but also in structure. Therefore, frankly, they can be either very good or nothing more than a mini-concert, the latter not really a method of instruction but more an overview demonstration. You will encounter both in your travels.

It must also be said that a great picker does not necessarily a great instructor make. Many of us have skills that we are good at, yet we are unable to convey them with ease to others. That being said, however, most musicians when approached by fans, and if not pressed for time, will spend a few minutes patiently showing you a particular lick or run.

Festival workshops can run from forty-five minutes up to perhaps two hours in length. Typically, there is a panel of "expert" instructors, for example, four different banjo players, perhaps Bill Keith, Tony Trischka, Alan Munde, and J.D. Crowe. Something of a dream team, right? Each of these has a distinctive technique or approach and, therefore, something a little different to contribute to a session on an individual basis. Usually this goes round-robin, where each, in turn, talks for a few minutes about his or her particular style or technique and perhaps who his or her influences were. Then each will likely play a short tune or passage to demonstrate. Optimally, a question-and-answer period is encouraged where audience members can ask specific questions regarding a technique or a particular move.

Size of workshops will affect the structure. In other words, at a large festival, a workshop as described above might attract fifty to a hundred on-lookers. Others might be focused at more manageably sized audiences, say twenty to thirty people, where each brings an instrument and will actually learn while playing along with the instructors. Here it is more likely that the instructors are limited to only one or two on stage or possibly set up in an intimate and informal semicircle. At the conclusion of such a workshop can be an ideal time to approach an artist to inquire about lessons or instructional materials, especially if you find you like this musician's style of teaching. Remember, patience and clear explanations are essential.

If you like the feel of festival workshops, perhaps extended workshops or camps are the next step for you. These can be full-day intensive, hands-on sessions or extended over a weekend or an entire week. A large number of "camps" have popped up in recent years. Most feature a bank of instructors who share teaching duties or from whom you might learn on a rotation basis as the days go along, providing the opportunity to obtain a variety of input and insight into different styles. Often the settings are "Y" camps or college campuses (during summer months) where cabin or dorm room accommodations are the norm. Fees vary widely, of course.

Some of these extended workshops and camps are not limited to bluegrass but might also offer Celtic fiddle styles or old-time (clawhammer) banjo, for example, among numerous other topics. In other words, many have become eclectic, offering a diversity of related genres and coursework.

And, finally, remember that many of these are not restricted to adults; some welcome children into the mix, while others host camps just for kids.

BLUEGRASS IN THE SCHOOLS

Several bluegrass school programs have been developed around the country successfully. Many bands either participate in a particular curriculum or touring presentation, or have children-specific programs they will perform when requested. Some belong to local chapters of the nationwide network Young Audiences (http://www.youngaudiences.com), which presents performing and visual artists to children, and is a good resource to assist in arranging a program with an appropriate bluegrass group.

The IBMA has available a school program-implementation manual and resource guide. Such agendas involve much more than simply inviting a bluegrass band to play for a school assembly. More like a mini-workshop, the presentation includes an overview of the history of bluegrass, an introduction to each instrument, as well as some performance and audience participation to further demonstrate the fun of the music.

Among several success stories is that of the Wheeling (West Virginia) Park High School's Bluegrass Club, started in 1992 out of concern for the direction lyrics were taking in popular commercial music. Its founder, Bob Turbanic, was honored by the IBMA in 2003 for this undertaking, about which he has also extended his knowledge and assistance to schools in fourteen other states. The Bluegrass Club now comprises four different bluegrass bands, one for each school level. Each group usually stays together as a unit for all four years of high school. The bands have performed in five states: Ohio, West Virginia, Pennsylvania, Kentucky, and Indiana. The club meets after school two to four days a week for two to three hours each, during which time the students are taught how to play. In addition, it is a year-round activity extending beyond the traditional school year.

Turbanic described the program further, as well as his motivation for it, in an interview we did in October 2003 in Louisville, Kentucky.

> We started out in '93 with three students. Now in 2003, we have close to a hundred students in the Bluegrass Club. We have four complete performing bands comprising almost thirty students. They go out and perform. For several years, we had a weekly radio show on our high school radio station. We hope to revive this when we get new equipment. We perform for assemblies; we perform all over our hometown. We're in the Yearbook. Kids bring their banjos to school with them on the bus. It's just another form of music. In Wheeling Park, because of the Bluegrass Club, the kids who like bluegrass are just considered like any other kid who just happened to like this particular music. There's no stereotype, there's no stigma attached to it. They aren't looked down on like a bunch of little hillbillies . . . it's just an accepted form of student music.
>
> Many people in America today complain that we are losing or have already lost traditional American culture…the traditional American morals and sense of values, sense of community with emphasis on home and faith and family. My contention is that bluegrass music and the culture that sustains it is the final repository of that in America. Bluegrass music is the only music that's culturally connected both in the theme of the music and the way that it's presented, how it's pursued, how it's taught. It is very much like that neighborhood, that family, that small community that we used to all have everywhere and that we all bemoan that we've lost. I believe that bluegrass music still has that and has it not only for people my age, but it has it for my kids.

I asked Turbanic what percentage of the students in the Bluegrass Club came from a home where bluegrass was encouraged as a result, perhaps, of having parents already involved or interested in bluegrass music. His response was quite surprising.

In the last ten years, two students. My daughter, who came from our family, of course, and we've always played bluegrass, and Amanda Kuwalski. I played in a bluegrass band with her uncle. Her family's involved in bluegrass. But ninety-nine percent of the kids coming in never have played a bluegrass instrument. Most of them don't even know what it is till they come to school. Now that is changing as we get better known and we get more and more of the students.

We're starting to now see students coming to our weekly jams that we hold after school, in the seventh grade, sixth grade, eighth grade because their older brothers were involved, their older sisters were involved. As a fraternal organization, we develop legacies. We're starting to get some legacies. We're reinstituting that sort of family tradition of coming up through the family and playing their music, but we're starting at the high school level and reaching down to the younger students.

Among those who started out young and are already in today's spotlight as teens and twenty-somethings are Malibu Storm's Shankman twins, Dana and Lauren, performing since age fourteen and award winners on banjo and fiddle, respectively; fiddler Casey Driessen, playing since age six and now in his mid-twenties and already teaching as well; award-winning flatpicker Cody Kilby, who went on to work with Ricky Skaggs and Kentucky Thunder; Casey Henry, who grew up surrounded by bluegrass since birth with mother–banjo teacher, Murphy Henry; and fiddle player Michael Cleveland, a major award winner and, by the time he was twenty-one, veteran of two top groups, Dale Ann Bradley and Coon Creek as well as Rhonda Vincent and the Rage.

There are numerous youngsters already making waves with their incredible talent. Young virtuosi seem to pop up as fast as I can type. Among precocious pickers and singers to watch for are Ryan Holladay, Michelle Porter, Tyler Andal, Molly Cherryholmes, Corey Walker, Sarah Jarosz, and Sierra Hull. Preteen Holladay, for example, first performed on the *Grand Ole Opry* at the age of five, the youngest ever on that program. He plays banjo, mandolin, guitar, and dobro, and has already recorded with Earl Scruggs.

Many of these musicians are graduates of the annual World of Bluegrass Fan Fest showcase of young talent. Organized by bluegrass veteran Pete Wernick, the Bluegrass Youth All Stars debuted in 1993 on the International Bluegrass Music Awards show. That lineup featured Chris Thile (mandolin), Michael Cleveland (fiddle), Cody Kilby (guitar), Josh Williams (banjo), and Brady Stogdill (bass). They went on to jam impromptu with legendary flatpicker Doc Watson. Each year, more and more "under twenty-one" names are added to this roster of up-and-comers.

HIGHER LEARNING

It isn't necessary to leave bluegrass behind upon high school graduation. Several colleges and universities now offer music programs that either incorporate bluegrass or have dedicated bluegrass curriculums. Most go further by including music business courses in the programs to prepare musicians more fully for a lifelong professional career.

Former successful students, for example, in the South Plains College (Levelland, Texas) creative arts program, which offers a bluegrass focus, include Ron Block of Union Station, Del McCoury Band bass player Mike Bub, and Dixie Chick Natalie Maines.

East Tennessee State University offers a bluegrass and country music program as well within its Center for Appalachian Studies and Services. Among its alumni are Mountain Heart's Adam Steffey, Blue Highway's Tim Stafford, and Barry Bales from Alison Krauss + Union Station. The program directors are veteran performers Jack Tottle and Raymond W. McLain.

Bluegrass Pride is the ETSU band. Over the years, with its many talented members, it has toured such countries as Russia, Belgium, and Japan, to name a few. In 2002, Taro Inoue was the band's mandolinist. He is the son of Saburo Watanabe Inoue, from Japan's legendary Bluegrass 45, discussed in chapter 8; bluegrass family circles extend to the international bluegrass family as well.

In October 2002, I asked the group's banjo player, J.P. Mathes, what the attraction for bluegrass should be for other young people. He responded, "It's an American art form. It's the most powerful type of music that I've ever found."

A WORD ABOUT INSTRUMENTS

Hundreds of manufacturers and independent luthiers build an enormous array of bluegrass instruments in the United States and in several other countries where bluegrass is popular. There is a lot to be said for instruments crafted either by mass production or singly in a small workshop. When considering an instrument for purchase, one must always look at overall workmanship as well as finances to be spent, placed in perspective to your abilities and intended use (professional vs. pleasure playing). However, most importantly, hold, play, and listen to the instrument before purchasing it. Take someone knowledgeable with you when making a purchase to help you assess quality. It cannot be stressed enough that how a particular instrument *sounds to you and feels to you* are the most important considerations. Pick it up, play it, pass it on!

11

On the Horizon

Traditional to progressive, there are hundreds of bluegrass acts around the country, around the world. The resources at the end of *Homegrown Music* will guide you to far more musicians than have been covered. In addition to the many artists mentioned throughout the book, here are just a handful of the more enduring performers who remain widely—if not wildly—popular among fans today. Many of them have claimed one or more industry awards over the years: Larry Stephenson Band, Blue Highway, Special Consensus, Rarely Herd, Lost and Found, and BlueRidge. A returnee to bluegrass is Marty Raybon, who spent a successful stint with country music's Shenandoah.

A plentiful selection of younger, emerging artists continues to grow in both traditional as well as progressive bluegrass camps. James Reams and the Barnstormers rely on early country material and originals written in authentic style. The results are a virtual history of the music and its roots, played in a clean, heartfelt manner that is somewhere between Monroe's and the Stanleys'. Nothin' Fancy represents one of the brightest progressive groups on today's scene, with thoughtful arrangements and an exceptional repertoire of original songs.

Award-winning Mountain Heart has been turning heads with its powerhouse gospel since the late nineties. The Steep Canyon Rangers secured first place in a prestigious band competition in 2001 and went on to land a record label deal in 2003, putting them on the fast track to an already promising career. Valerie Smith and Liberty Pike have become festival favorites in the few short years since they formed. In addition to Smith's dynamic voice, Becky Buller's expertise on an array of instruments adds punch to their lively performances.

One of the more interesting stories behind the making of a band is that of Cherryholmes. A family band first initiated in 1999, they packed up and put into storage their possessions, then took to the road in 2002, traveling in their bus around the country. Since then, they have appeared on the *Grand Ole Opry*, have released a new recording produced by Darrin Vincent, and garnered a group of the year award in 2004.

Among other performers attracting tremendous attention as spring 2004 was in view are King Wilkie, David Peterson and 1946, the Gibson Brothers, Pine Mountain Railroad, Open Road, Kenny and Amanda Smith, and singer Alecia Nugent, whose vibrant voice positions her to turn to a wide range of bluegrass as well as crossover projects. Yonder Mountain String Band, Railroad Earth, and Robinella and the CCstringband each use bluegrass as a springboard but expand from there. Two of the most popular alternative fringe groups whose performances exhibit bluegrass influences are Leftover Salmon and String Cheese Incident.

In the tradition of former "kid" superpickers Alison Krauss and Mark O'Connor, multi-instrumentalist Sierra Hull is poised to step into the spotlight, actually, step further into a spotlight that is already shining on her.

When I first met and spoke with Sierra in the fall of 2002, she had just shown multiple Grammy winner Ricky Skaggs a mandolin lick or two on stage. Then eleven years old, she already exhibited a remarkably confident stage presence, polite and intelligent interview skills, as well as jaw-dropping talent.

Adam Steffey, mandolin player for Mountain Heart and former sideman with Alison Krauss + Union Station, commented to me as Sierra came off the stage: "I think she's the future of this music, and all the young folks like her are just unreal. I wish I had started playing at that age. I hear folks like that and it just makes me want to put mine [mandolin] up and just weep," he said, laughing. "Remember that name! She is awesome."

Sierra represents a rapidly expanding pool of promising young musicians who have new choices in the twenty-first century of how and where to learn to play bluegrass music, not only for fun, but also as a lifelong professional career.

SIERRA HULL: REMEMBER THAT NAME!

"I love bluegrass. My name is Sierra Dawn Hull. I just turned eleven."

With these words, sound check was concluded for this interview, conducted minutes after Sierra Hull had played mandolin on stage alongside

Ricky Skaggs. Her challenging chops invited a quick and rousing audience reaction and sent many photographers scrambling for a photo op.

Since that time, she has quickly gained recognition and continues to rack up impressive accomplishments. Sierra has appeared on the *Grand Ole Opry*, on CMT with Alison Krauss, as well as on the latest PBS *All-Star Bluegrass Celebration*. She has jammed not only with the best but also with the legendary, from Sam Bush to Earl Scruggs. In addition, she and her family have established a festival, the Sierra Hull Bluegrass Festival, held in September in their home town of Byrdstown, Tennessee.

Spring 2004 found her working on her first release for Rounder Records. Adding to her excitement, she was preparing to participate, along with brother Cody, on the T Bone Burnett–produced *Great High Mountain Tour*, a celebration of the music from *O Brother, Where Art Thou?*, *Down from the Mountain*, and *Cold Mountain*. Sierra and Cody Hull would be joining Alison Krauss + Union Station with Jerry Douglas, Ralph Stanley, the Nashville Bluegrass Band, and the Whites, to name only a few.

In spite of her rapid rise to national recognition, Sierra remains grounded and centered at home in Tennessee, where she has "a lot of fun" and loves to be around her friends at school (according to her Web page bio, which she wrote!).

Sierra was charming, responding to questions in unadulterated Southern "kid speak." She exhibited a tremendous precocity in her demeanor and in her thoughtful, future-minded answers.

SPL: How did you get involved in bluegrass?

SH: My dad had this mandolin, and he was actually trying to learn. I got to liking bluegrass because of him. I got to seeing my Uncle Junior play a fiddle. And I remember seeing him since I was little. I asked my granny about the fiddle, so she got me one for Christmas. I got to seeing that everything on a fiddle was the same as on the mandolin. You can just basically convert what you learn on the mandolin to the fiddle. Then I decided that I got to playing the mandolin more, and I enjoy it a lot more than the fiddle. It's just to me a lot funner instrument.

SPL: How long have you been playing?

SH: About three years, playing since I was eight. At Smithville [Fiddlers' Jamboree], I've been in a bunch of competitions. Last year at Smithville, I won first on the guitar and second on the mandolin, the Guitar National Championship Beginners. This year I went back and I won first place on the national guitar [championship] and first place on the mandolin.

SPL: Did your dad "push" you toward bluegrass or did you just really like it when you first heard it?

SH: He was going to a bunch of broken down schoolhouses, I mean, where they jammed just about every weekend. We still go there all the time. As I was getting more involved and playing in music, I was going with him more. I'm from a little town called Byrdstown, Tennessee.

SPL: Do you have a lot of friends your own age who play bluegrass?

SH: Well, like, at school I'll be talking about bluegrass. And I'm sure they're thinking, "Oh, I hate hearing her talk about that so much." But as far as people, I guess I met most of my friends right here [at World of Bluegrass] that are more my age. Because around where I live, nobody really plays music, as far as kids. I'm about the only kid that plays, me and my brother.

SPL: Have you tried to turn your friends on to bluegrass?

SH: Yeah, I've talked to my friends a lot about it, but I don't think they're really that interested.

SPL: How would you convince them that bluegrass is great music?

SH: Well, they've heard me play. I've played at school a lot. They think it's cool. They don't think it's stupid or anything like that. But as far as trying to learn, I think a lot of it has to do with their parents, because their parents have to be kind of involved in it with them. My mom and dad have been taking me to places for a long time where I can learn and become a better picker. But a lot of kids' parents, I don't think, would go out of their way to do that much for them. And I think that has a lot to do with it.

SPL: What grade are you in?

SH: I'm in the sixth grade this year.

SPL: And what do you want to be when you grow up?

SH: I want to be a mu*si*cian. *(This was stated very confidently and emphatically, with emphasis on the second syllable.)*

SPL: Do you want to go to a college where they will teach you not only about the music but also about the business of music?

SH: I think a lot ahead. I've been thinking and I would really love to try and get a scholarship, if I could, to go play and then study music, bluegrass.

SPL: Only bluegrass or other music, too?

SH: I think like Chris Thile [of Nickel Creek]. He plays a lot of different kinds of music. I don't think what he plays is really bluegrass. But a lot of things like that I enjoy. I think he's studied classical; you can tell it in his playing. I'd kind of like to be a fuller musician, rather than just caught in bluegrass. You can always go back to bluegrass. If you learn the different types of music, you can go back and it will help you a lot in your bluegrass. And that's something a lot of people don't have.

SPL: Tell me about your brother.

SH: Cody Hull. He's just been playing electric bass here lately for us, for about two or three months. He didn't like bluegrass that much to begin with, but I think now that we've been practicing around the house, I think he's growing to it a little bit more. And I think that's what I'm going to have to do with my friends. You've got to grow into this stuff. Once you hear it, you'll love it.

SPL: Do you have a band with your brother?

SH: At Pine Haven Community Center, I usually get Loyle Logan to play fiddle for me and Ronnie Gilreath. And they are the people that played on my CD. Carl Berggren—he used to teach me mandolin for about six months—played the guitar. Ronnie Gilreath plays the banjo. Loyle Logan plays the fiddle, Sandy Gerkins plays the bass, and I play the mandolin. And I play the guitar on one song.

When we first met, Sierra had just released her first self-produced recording entitled Angel Mountain. *She talked about her future recording plans.*

SH: I'm not on a record label. I hope to be some day. I think it'd be kind of neat. I'm hoping my next [CD] will be better. I'm going to work on another one over the winter. The one I have out right now is an all-instrumental album. I'm hoping to have one with singing and get Cody to sing some on it and things like that.

SPL: Do both of you sing?

SH: Yeah, we do a lot of harmony. And most of the time, he does the lead and I'll lead on something. We just kind of switch out.

SPL: How did you meet Ricky Skaggs?

SH: I'm going to be playing at the young kids thing, Amazing Kids workshop. We were all playing in there [backstage green room]. Actually, Adam Steffey walked by and I couldn't help it; I had to go meet him.

He's like a hero; I had to go meet him. Then Ricky Skaggs walked in. Then John Laswell [workshop coordinator] said, "I want you to meet somebody [Ricky]." And we started playing. And he [Ricky] just asked me if I would get up there and pick one with him. He's a hero, too.

Interview conducted October 18, 2002, Bluegrass Fan Fest, Galt House, Louisville, Kentucky.

12

Down the Road: Continuing the Tradition

In recent years, I had occasion to visit two nonbluegrass music museums, the Rock and Roll Hall of Fame and Museum in Cleveland and the Country Music Hall of Fame in Nashville. At both spaces, I found it fascinating to see the lineage for each music laid out in timelines and in exhibits. Tracing the genres through their origins and influences clearly demonstrated how inextricably intertwined music styles are and that no music is insular. From simple, unadorned roots that began with ballads, hymns, and fiddle tunes to blues laments and soulful acoustic guitar work, many musics, in fact, grew from the same garden of mixed seeds.

It was satisfying to see bluegrass given due recognition in both houses. A twentieth-century music, born in the United States, bluegrass was cultivated by a combination of social circumstance, cultural traditions, and ingenuity. And it relied upon the same unembellished beginnings as others.

These tangled vines are the very ones that will ensure the preservation of bluegrass. They are hearty, rooted deep within the fabric of America's music. They are nurtured by each successive generation of enthusiasts and players. Each rediscovers what is old, thereby making it new again.

Bluegrass music is a tradition that remains as exciting and inventive as the younger players that contribute to its continuation. Moreover, whether we modernize it, augment it, or blend it with a diversity of sounds and influences, it retains its value by virtue of its core makeup.

To consider its future, one must ponder the future of all music. With technology changing and advancing at a speed unimaginable a few short years ago, and with laws being challenged and changed not quite as rapidly as these "modern" advancements, one has to wonder how we will be enjoying our music in the future.

DVD technology has already rendered videotape products obsolete. Furthermore, it is fast replacing CDs as more and more performers opt to include video, in addition to audio, on their releases. Internet music downloads have become popular and accessible so rapidly that laws pertaining to copyright infringement, music licensing rights, and royalties are not yet firmly in place to protect all parties. Once these issues and other challenges brought on by new technology are addressed appropriately, we are sure to see new methods of music dissemination, be they for audio recordings or live video performance.

It has already been speculated that, in the not-so-distant future, "hard copy" audio and visual recordings will disappear from view altogether. Music purchases will rely entirely on Internet downloads, direct to home devices for computer, car, home entertainment center, personal audio, and others. Can't get to a concert because the distance is too far? Streaming live performances will become standard, along with the ability to capture and save them to permanent media for replay. Sure, there will be fees involved, but music will be even simpler to access than it already is.

Greater opportunities to share music, including bluegrass, will arrive as continuing advances are made in technology. Especially for what are considered "niche" genres, this can only be a positive outcome. Bluegrass has not yet reached a level of commercial viability in the greater population. Therefore, the ability to share bluegrass on a wider plane—and more cost effectively—via such media as Internet and satellite radio will aid in its future prospects.

These advances can offer novel, as well as improved, opportunities for bluegrass enthusiasts. It widens the circle to share information about exciting new groups. Perhaps you will take an interactive banjo lesson online. How about video conferencing a jam session with friends across an ocean?

While some might argue that if all music goes the way of computers, how can this be good for bluegrass? I think the answer lies within the music itself. Bluegrass is a gregarious music by its very nature. We want to reach out to other bluegrassers. The Internet and other advanced technology will provide additional methods to do so; they will not be replacements. Bluegrass will remain very much a hands-on, participatory genre. Furthermore, the more bluegrass proliferates via new technology, the more we will experience an increase in the live, in-person activities available.

With a larger fan base will come greater diversity in the sound of bluegrass. It will gain more bends and blends as music in general continues to age and evolve. There will be groups like Nickel Creek who will learn from bluegrass and who will smile back on that education as they open new, as yet unimagined, doors of music.

Music is a continuum, ever changing but always relying on its past to ensure its future. Music has to change to some degree to remain fresh. Rock-and-roll has not remained static, yet there remains rock-and-roll.

By the same token, there will be tradition bearers who will continue to pass on to their children, and on to the next generations, the hallmarks of the music. We already have the next generation of our most prominent musicians passing the torch to their children. Bill Monroe, Earl Scruggs, and Ralph Stanley have been joined previously in music by their children. Today, for example, we have Del McCoury as well as Ricky Skaggs and his wife, Sharon White, looking to the future of bluegrass in their own children.

Bluegrass must be passed along. The future of bluegrass is in the hands of the children. Introduce them to bluegrass. Let them hear it played by other youngsters. Make opportunities available and attractive to them to hear and enjoy the music. Younger people are open to new sounds; if they were not, the Beatles or Britney would not have made it into the lexicon. It is critical that youngsters see and hear other youngsters playing bluegrass; these are their best role models because then they will turn to you and say, "Mom, Dad, will you buy me a banjo?"

Music culturally enriches our lives and the lives of our children. The talent and artistry it cultivates is precious. It also brightens the lives of our senior citizens and soothes the infirmed. Let the vibrancy and soul of great bluegrass speak for itself. Its voice is louder than we realize if we only let it out more often.

To paraphrase Emmylou Harris's words that opened chapter 2, to know where the future of bluegrass is headed, we must embrace and nurture its past. In it will be reflected the enduring simplicity of a music that comes straight from the heart, goes straight to the heart, and is full of spirit and soul.

On September 2, 1983, I asked Bill Monroe what his thoughts were on the future of bluegrass. His response was emphatic and simple: "Bluegrass is growing every day; it's still growing."

The music itself is its future. Bluegrass is a timeless tradition. By appreciating bluegrass for its intrinsic value, we can safeguard it, nurture it, enjoy it to the fullest. With such comprehension and care, bluegrass will continue to be a colorful, vibrant thread in the fabric of our lives in America and a cultural treasure to be shared around the globe.

Afterword: Rediscovering Bluegrass

Researching and writing this book became a completely unexpected rediscovery of bluegrass for me. I found it deeply emotional to revisit old friends as I watched videos I had not seen previously or in a long while, pored over vinyl record albums (yes, remember them!?) and older CDs that I had not listened to in some cases for years (not difficult when one's collection is close to 3,000), read brand new books, and leafed through and reviewed old ones.

The process took on the feel of a new beginning, a new understanding for me. I became a newcomer to bluegrass once again in a way that was much different from my initial introduction to the music when I was thrust into it, essentially out of a desire to earn a paycheck, three decades ago.

Most of the resources relied on or looked to for *Homegrown Music: Discovering Bluegrass* did not exist when I first became professionally involved in 1975. It is satisfying to know how much the music and its resources have grown since that time. You are fortunate to have the opportunity to benefit from this expansion.

I was humbled and awed the more I realized, or perhaps was reawakened to, the legendary status and profound importance of the very many people I have been privileged to have met and known along the way. When we work within a chosen field, we often take for granted those treasures among us. Sometimes and somehow, we do not appreciate them in as special a light as they deserve.

I would like to take a moment to acknowledge those often overlooked in discussions of bluegrass, all the behind-the-scenes personnel. Bluegrass, as any other form of music, could not survive and thrive without those who run the sound boards, mix the recordings, produce events, "spin" the CDs, book the artists, write about and generate the publicity for bluegrass and its musicians, build the instruments, run the many fan-based clubs and associations, and volunteer for any task needed.

To everyone who is a part of the bluegrass family, thanks for creating and preserving homegrown music.

Twenty-Five Recordings to Jump-Start Your Collection ... Plus a Random Sampling of Videos

These twenty-five treasures represent a broad spectrum. Some are historically important recordings, while others are by cream-of-the-crop contemporary artists. This is not a "must have" or a "best recordings" list. It does not include all the important pioneers, just as it cannot include all the most popular current performers. This is a completely subjective list, one that contains recordings that I believe you will not only enjoy but that will also lead you to others. Therefore, consider these as introductions to the wide world of bluegrass. The further you travel on your bluegrass journey, the more you will want to add to your bluegrass collection.

Those already immersed in bluegrass should find it delightful to revisit some of the older recordings or those recently reissued on CD. Readers are encouraged to pursue albums by other artists mentioned in this book, particularly the younger performers whose musicianship seems to improve with each new group that emerges.

A plethora of compilations is widely available that offers the opportunity to sample a particular style, theme, or instrument focus. Comprehensive boxed sets covering the careers of some of bluegrass music's pioneers will prove rewarding as you become more familiar with, and develop a stronger appreciation for, the finer points of bluegrass.

Listen with an open mind; the recordings listed here are certainly not the last word in bluegrass. There is an ocean of pearls out there and why not, given the long history of this exceptional music where excellence and virtuosity are hallmarks. I think you will find these choices great starting points to familiarize you with—and get you excited about—discovering bluegrass.

Kenny Baker. *Frost on the Pumpkin* **(County 2731)**

Kenny Baker is looked to as the quintessential bluegrass fiddler, having spent more years as a Blue Grass Boy than any other. His style is smooth, fluid, relaxed, and his exceptional mastery shines on this recording, first released in the mid-seventies. The album represents a delightful blend of standard tunes and originals.

Berline-Crary-Hickman. *Chambergrass: A Decade of Tunes from the Edges of Bluegrass* **(Sugar Hill 3945)**

This is an all-instrumental showcase of just how far bluegrass can be stretched, infused with a variety of genre influences and played with exceptional virtuosity. From straightforward traditional fiddle tunes (toyed with expertly) by Byron Berline to John Hickman's banjo meeting the challenge, both woven around flatpicking innovator Dan Crary's guitar, the numbers are creatively bent in the many directions of the trio's influences.

The Country Gentlemen. *Folk Songs and Bluegrass*
(Smithsonian Folkways 40022)

First released in 1961, this album introduced what was to become known as the "Classic" Country Gentlemen sound, that of Charlie Waller, John Duffey, Eddie Adcock, and Tom Gray. Each an innovator in his own right, the individuals eventually went on to other groundbreaking bands, except for Waller who remains at the helm today. With a decidedly urban influence, the "Gents" were leaders in the "progressive" bluegrass movement, injecting novel banjo moves from Adcock, an artful bass approach by Gray, and high harmony vocals with a definitive edge from Waller and Duffey, the latter who also approached mandolin with a special flair.

J.D. Crowe and the New South. *Live in Japan* **(Rounder 0159)**

There are a handful of banjo players within bluegrass who each developed unique styles by fusing bluegrass with such genres as jazz, rock, or classical; Crowe is one of those pioneers. This concert performance captures him with a prolific lineup of sidemen: the magnetic voice of Keith Whitley, driving fiddle from Bobby Slone, avant-garde mandolinist Jimmy Gaudreau, and Steve Bryant backing it all up on electric bass.

Hazel Dickens and Alice Gerrard. *Pioneering Women of Bluegrass*
(Smithsonian Folkways 40065)

Comprised of their first two albums, this release is pivotal in demonstrating the role women have played in bluegrass, one often overshadowed and overlooked by male counterparts in the music's early history and whose role only came of age in the late eighties and into the nineties. Supporting musicians include, among others, mandolinist David Grisman, fiddlers Chubby Wise and Billy Baker, and Lamar Grier on banjo. The duo's vivacious vocals go through the paces on numbers from the Stanley Brothers, the Carter Family, and Bill Monroe. Detailed liner notes by historian-folklorist Neil Rosenberg, Dickens, and Gerrard provide further insight into Hazel and Alice's significance.

Flatt and Scruggs at Carnegie Hall! The Complete Concert (Koch 7929)

Key players while in Bill Monroe's band who would help cement the "Monroe" bluegrass sound, Lester and Earl went on to introduce banjo and bluegrass music to popular culture by way of television's *The Beverly Hillbillies*. Step back in time to hear the warmth of the music in a live setting on one of the world's most prestigious—and best acoustic—stages. The duo's enduring sound is unmatched even today.

The Greenbriar Boys. *The Best of the Vanguard Years* (Vanguard 206/207)

Based in New York City's Greenwich Village and riding the tide of the sixties' folk boom, the Greenbriar Boys played a pivotal role in the development of bluegrass and its popularity in the Northeast. The group's cosmopolitan perspective broadened the bluegrass audience and had a tremendous impact on bridging the "urban-rural" gap. This CD features songwriter-vocalist John Herald, banjo picker Bob Yellin, and folklorist-mandolinist Ralph Rinzler. Frank Wakefield, who later replaced Rinzler, is also heard on this collection.

John Hartford. *Aereo-Plain* (Rounder 0366)

From the extensive catalog of one of music's most complex creative artists, this classic album features mostly original songs and tunes by Hartford, who is heard on banjo and guitar. He is accompanied by a stellar stable of musicians—Norman Blake, Tut Taylor, Vassar Clements, Randy Scruggs—who complement each others' playing seamlessly.

Hot Rize. *So Long of a Journey* (Sugar Hill 3943)

Sparkling banjo, guitar, and vocals, as well as beautifully constructed originals set this band apart when they emerged on the bluegrass scene in 1978. Disbanding after more than a decade as one of the most popular groups on the bluegrass circuit, the group reconvened in 1996 for a reunion concert in Boulder, Colorado, where it was secretly taped and appears here as a wonderful testament to their talent, especially poignant because guitarist Charles Sawtelle passed away three years later.

The Jim and Jesse Story. 24 Greatest Hits (CMH 9022)

A generous selection of the legendary McReynolds brothers' best known songs, this album spans their eclectic repertoire, from traditional archives to rockabilly, and includes John Prine's powerful "Paradise." Jesse's cross-picking mandolin set standards, while the harmony vocals with sibling Jim could rival those of the Everly Brothers.

The Johnson Mountain Boys. *At the Old Schoolhouse* (Rounder 0260)

Acknowledged as one of the greatest traditional bands to have ever toured in contemporary times, the Johnson Mountain Boys captured exquisitely all the critical elements that are the foundation of Monroe-style bluegrass. They exhibited instrumental virtuosity, rapid precision playing, tight harmonies, bone-chilling a cappella gospel renderings, and that high lonesome vocal sound. Meant as a farewell concert, this energetic live album garnered a Grammy nomination and the first IBMA Album of the Year nod.

King Wilkie. *Broke* (Rebel 1802)

From a twenty-first century band, this is a knock-out release for King Wilkie, a Virginia-based, all twenty-something ensemble. Their youth shines through in the punch and delivery of Monroe-style bluegrass as good as it can get. About half are originals that already sound old, that is, in the tradition, and will surely stand the test of time. King Wilkie represents superbly the second generation of neo-traditionalists. The recording pairs perfectly with the above-mentioned Johnson Mountain Boys' CD.

Alison Krauss + Union Station. *Live* (Rounder 0515)

The first ever live recording for Krauss and her equally talented crew, this CD draws on two concerts in Louisville in 2002. Twenty-five numbers cover many hits, three original Jerry Douglas tunes, and one traditional instrumental. This is a tremendous retrospective displaying the breadth and depth of these award-winning musicians. The real treat is hearing first-hand, through the intimacy of an "in person" recording, the energy and heart put into each song.

Jim Lauderdale & Ralph Stanley. *I Feel Like Singing Today* (Rebel 1755)

Contemporary and traditional meet on this award-winning CD, featuring old-time bluegrass woven from songs old and new. Lauderdale, one of the finest singer-songwriters primarily known in country music markets, works seamlessly with died-in-the-wool legend Ralph Stanley. To hear how Lauderdale can take a new song and make it traditional is a lesson in itself.

Doyle Lawson and Quicksilver. *Just Over in Heaven* (Sugar Hill 3911)

It is rare to find vocal harmonizing that can match, let alone surpass, that of Lawson backed by Quicksilver. Through the years, his recordings seem to expand on the concept of "outstanding." This all-gospel album blends the best of bluegrass gospel, Southern gospel, and contemporary Christian sounds, throwing in a hint of swing for good measure. The CD will move your musical spirit in new directions.

The Del McCoury Band. *A Deeper Shade of Blue* (Rounder 0303)

Although Del, a former sideman for Bill Monroe, has been heading up his own band for decades, his success and popularity were given a huge boost post–*O Brother, Where Art Thou?* when he took part in the sold-out "Down from the Mountain" concert tours. All top-notch, award-winning musicians, Del and "the Boys" have a special knack for making the most of the "blue(s)" in any bluegrass song.

Bill Monroe and the Bluegrass Boys. *Live Recordings 1956-1969:* *Off the Record Volume 1*

Bill Monroe and Doc Watson. *Live Duet Recordings 1963-1980:* *Off the Record Volume 2* (Smithsonian Folkways 40063 and 40064)

Okay, so this is really two CDs, but it is difficult to separate them in terms of intrinsic value for your collection. There are many compilations and boxed sets available covering the long career of Bill Monroe, and Watson has his own extensive library of releases. I have chosen these companion volumes for inclusion because the live aspect, for one, offers a glimpse into "Big Mon's" persona, on and off stage. The cuts were taken from many different sources ranging from the first ever weekend-long bluegrass festival in Fincastle, Virginia, to Fiddlin' Tex Logan's house in New Jersey. Second, the time period covers several different Blue Grass Boys configurations; here, it is interesting to note that on only one cut do we hear from fiddler Kenny Baker, who held that post with Monroe's band for more years than any other. Next, there is the rare opportunity, in a ten-minute segment, to hear Monroe joined by brothers Birch and Charlie.

Finally, with Volume 2 comes the opportunity to hear two masters in spare duet, much in the way Bill began in the early days with brother Charlie. Bill and Doc are wonderfully complementary, each bringing into the picture songs that capture the roots and the essence of bluegrass and traditional music. Cap this set off with comprehensive liner notes from folklorist Ralph Rinzler, and you will find you have joyfully experienced a textbook's worth of music and information.

The Lynn Morris Band. *Mama's Hand* (Rounder 0328)

The title cut, from the pen of Hazel Dickens, was the IBMA Song of the Year in 1996. Lynn Morris consistently cuts recordings that capture the spirit of bluegrass and old-time music in a warm, compelling manner. Selection of songs, including band member originals, always covers some of the music's best composers, as it does in this exceptional release.

Nashville Bluegrass Band. *To Be His Child* (Rounder 0242)

A groundbreaking gospel release from a rock-steady band that has been around since the mid-1980s, *To Be His Child* remains a selection to return to time and again for a powerfully emotional lift. With an amazing repertoire, the Nashville Bluegrass Band approaches its material, be it sacred or secular, much like the street singing style that doo-wop drew from in the fifties. The group's precision a cappella harmonizing chills to the bone and can bring a tear to the eye.

New Grass Revival. *On the Boulevard* (Sugar Hill 3745)

Leaders of the progressive bluegrass movement, bold enough to declare themselves as such in the band name, New Grass Revival set new standards, not without controversy, for its clear infusion of electric rock and jazz with traditional bluegrass. Various personnel came and went; this CD's configuration spawned internationally acclaimed Béla Fleck, who likely rivals Earl Scruggs, albeit in a different light, for renown on banjo.

Old and In the Way. *That High Lonesome Sound* (Acoustic Disc 19)

This unusual gathering of musical minds was revolutionary in its original heyday. Here, Grateful Dead founder Jerry Garcia on banjo teams up with jazz-grass mandolinist David "Dawg" Grisman, renegade singer-songwriter Peter Rowan, "hillbilly jazz" fiddler Vassar Clements, and Dead bassist John Kahn for a live recording from 1973. The bluegrass that resulted is like no other.

Ricky Skaggs and Tony Rice. *The Essential Old-Time Country Duet Recordings* (Sugar Hill 3711)

With the simplicity of unadorned mandolin and guitar and perfectly matched harmonies, Skaggs and Rice reflect on the duet "brother" sound upon which bluegrass was built. The selections are graceful and compelling gems, all of which are mainstays in today's traditional bluegrass catalog.

The Seldom Scene. *Live at the Cellar Door* (Rebel 1103)

The "Scene" urbanized bluegrass like no other. When this recording was released originally in 1975, it became a classic almost instantly—as it remains today. John Duffey, Mike Auldridge, John Starling, Ben Eldridge, and Tom Gray are heard in their prime on this album, enhanced by the fact that it is a live performance.

Skyline with Tony Trischka. *Ticket Back: A Retrospective* (Flying Fish 664)

Banjo has been experimented with and stretched far beyond the bonds of bluegrass. One such banjo innovator is Tony Trischka. The "master" at whose knee Béla Fleck learned, Trischka, accompanied by Skyline—Barry Mitterhoff, Dan Weiss, Larry Cohen, Dede Wyland, and later Rachel Kalem taking Wyland's spot—set a new standard for ensemble playing. As a New York–based band, the urban effects could be heard; nothing held back their bright, contemporary, sophisticated sound. This is a compilation CD of some of their best and most popular material, including the title track penned by Martha Trachtenberg, founding member of the first all-women bluegrass group, the Buffalo Gals.

IIIrd Tyme Out. *John and Mary* (Rounder 0463)

Voted Vocal Group of the Year, among other honors, many times over by peers and fans, IIIrd Tyme Out demonstrates a pure, simple, and smooth approach to bluegrass that has staying power. This dynamic band artfully places contemporary and traditional bluegrass in counterpoint to each other, resulting in a winning mix with every song that comes its way.

RARE FINDS

Two out-of-print chestnuts are well worth combing through the vintage bins (CD or vinyl) at flea markets or festivals; if you find them, grab 'em quick:

The Kentucky Colonels (with Roland and Clarence White).
Appalachian Swing! **(Rounder SS31)**

This is a treasure of twelve instrumentals that epitomizes the beauty and expression of bluegrass music's tempo and demeanor. Recorded forty years ago, without today's fancier, more sophisticated technology and without any overdubs, the purity of the music stands on its own like no other. Clarence White's guitar playing on this recording is often cited as a critical moment in the development of bluegrass flatpicking style. *Note: You might also stumble across this in vinyl format as The Kentucky Colonels featuring Roland and Clarence White, United Artists 29514 (an import).*

Norman Blake, Tut Taylor, Sam Bush, Butch Robins, Vassar Clements,
Dave Holland, Jethro Burns **(Flying Fish HDS 701)**

This collector's item showcases some of the most instrumental instrumentalists (pun intended) ever to have touched the bluegrass-and-beyond world. Each was an architect of fascinating approaches to the music, some in jazz directions. Bassist Holland is, in fact, a jazz musician whose credits include Miles Davis, Chick Corea, and Herbie Hancock, to name a few. Burns was one-half of the country comedy duo Homer and Jethro and was a major proponent of bringing mandolin to jazz stages.

VIDEO: A RANDOM SAMPLING

While a respectable number of videos has been released over the years, this medium seems to be just now coming of age in bluegrass. DVD is quickly replacing VHS format, and a handful of artists are beginning to issue companion CDs and DVDs simultaneously. New technology continues to bring back to life decades-old footage once thought lost forever.

A vast audio-visual catalog of instructional material, as well as numerous works old and new, including documentaries, biographies, concerts, and festivals, exists. In addition to *High Lonesome: The Story of Bluegrass Music*, listed in "Where to from Here" and those mentioned in "Selected Works Consulted," the following are examples of the broad spectrum available.

Bill Monroe: Father of Bluegrass Music **(Winstar, DVD and VHS)**

Renowned filmmaker Steve Gebhardt comprehensively chronicles the life and music of Monroe. John Hartford and Ricky Skaggs interview "Big Mon," while numerous former sidemen provide anecdotes and reminisce about time spent in the Blue Grass Boys. Several performance clips are included, as is a rare personal interview with "King of Country Music," Roy Acuff.

Bluegrass Jamming: A Guide for Newcomers and Closet Pickers Taught by Pete Wernick (Homespun, DVD and VHS)

Banjo innovator and seasoned instructor Pete Wernick provides an easy-going format for novices to learn the basics of playing together. He offers insider tips, such as how to know when a song is about to wrap up, when a chord is about to change, and so on. Lyrics and music to more than a dozen bluegrass standards are included. Learners are encouraged to play along.

Bluegrass Journey: A Documentary (Blue Stores, DVD and VHS)

Producers-directors Ruth Oxenberg and Rob Schumer take a look at the contemporary bluegrass scene via performance sequences and interviews, filmed primarily in 2000 at the annual IBMA World of Bluegrass and the Grey Fox Bluegrass Festival in upstate New York, with additional footage shot in 2002 in Kentucky.

Don Reno and Red Smiley and the Tennessee Cut-Ups: The Early Years (Pinecastle, VHS)

For a vintage perspective of the music, go back in time with narrator-historian Eddie Stubbs as he guides you through early performances from this influential group. Rare black-and-white television footage features not only Reno and Smiley but also an appearance by Ralph and Carter Stanley.

Down from the Mountain: A Film Celebrating the Music from the Movie O Brother, Where Art Thou? (Artisan Entertainment, DVD and VHS)

A docu-concert codirected by famed documentarians D.A. Pennebaker, Chris Hegedus, and Nick Doob, the video preserves the behind-the-scenes goings-on as well as the May 2000 concert that took place at Nashville's Ryman Auditorium. Such artists as Emmylou Harris, Alison Krauss, and John Hartford, among others, gathered to present a program of traditional music related to or featured in the Coen Brothers' epic that later went on to win a host of awards for its music, as did the soundtrack for this film.

King of Bluegrass: The Life and Times of Jimmy Martin (Straight Six Films, DVD and VHS)

The camera follows Jimmy Martin back stage and on tour, as well as at home, including one of his famed raccoon hunting trips and a handful of performance clips. He talks casually about his long, colorful career. Ralph Stanley, Tom T. Hall, Marty Stuart, J.D. Crowe, Paul Williams, Bill Emerson and others are also interviewed.

Muleskinner Live: The Video (Sierra, VHS)

Videotaped before a live audience in 1973, this historic concert was brought back to life nearly twenty years after the fact, when the once lost original was found. The band was an ensemble of young, hot-shot pickers in California who were originally scheduled simply to play a tribute opening set for their mentor, Bill Monroe, and then later to join in for a finale with Bill and his Blue Grass Boys. Three were former Blue Grass Boys them-selves, Richard Greene, Bill Keith, and Peter Rowan. David Grisman and Clarence White, two more moving forces in bluegrass and cutting edge acoustic, joined them. Monroe was a no-show due to a bus breakdown, and the five went on to do the whole program themselves. What makes this video all the more precious was the tragic death of prolific flatpicker White just months later.

Pickin' on 30 Years: Walnut Valley Festival and National Flatpicking Championship, 1972-2001
(VHS, http://www.wvfest.com)

A long popular, eclectic Kansas festival, "Winfield," as it is informally called, is internationally known as a "picker's paradise." In addition to numerous featured performers on four formal stages, competitions are held for guitar, mandolin, and dulcimer, to name a few. Byron Berline Band, Jim Hurst and Missy Raines, and Fragment from the Czech Republic are among the bluegrass artists who appear.

The Three Pickers: Earl Scruggs, Doc Watson, Ricky Skaggs (Rounder, DVD)

Scruggs and Watson, two legendary national treasures joined by a three-decades younger Skaggs, a shoe-in for similar status in another twenty or so years, is one of the best concepts ever captured on video. The music is exceptional and digs deep into bluegrass and its roots. Each presents segments with his respective bands or picking partners; Alison Krauss also guests. Wonderful brief biographies are provided, as are candid interviews.

Yo-Yo Ma, Edgar Meyer, Mark O'Connor: Appalachian Journey (Sony, **DVD and VHS)**

This April 2000 sold-out Lincoln Center concert provides a whole other perspective of bluegrass. Original classical and jazz compositions blend with traditional fiddle tunes, fired up by O'Connor's fiddling, reminiscent of his teenage days as a bluegrass and Texas-style fiddle champion. Intimate camera angles catch world-renowned cello master Ma and versatile bassist-composer Meyer sharing with O'Connor their variations on tradition. Onstage stories and backstage interviews provide fascinating insight. Guest appearances by fiddler-vocalist Alison Krauss and singer James Taylor are a plus.

Where to from Here:
Suggested Resources

The following recommendations will assist in your further exploration of bluegrass. Each offers either an immediate source or the road to others that are more detailed or specific to a particular interest. Many are supplementary to another, for example, those that deal with the music's origins and fringes.

Consider these the basis for an ongoing process of discovery. An Internet or library search will readily provide a stunning selection for further study. In addition to comprehensive histories and general overviews of bluegrass and its origins, there are numerous print and video biographies about key personalities. Rare footage continues to be restored of early twentieth-century progenitors of the music as technology opens doors to a look back at the past. While video documentaries exist about some of bluegrass music's major figures, younger artists are finding new outlets for up-to-date personal information. For example, some are producing performance DVDs that contain extended tracks with such features as interviews, photographs, or behind-the-scenes clips. Most living artists, or their record labels, maintain Internet sites with in-depth histories, discographies, and tour dates.

In choosing resources, keep in mind what it is you are looking to learn or from what perspective. Some items present an academic treatment, while others take a layman's approach.

Unlike thirty years ago, when competition was just kicking in within the business of bluegrass, there exists today a plethora of materials and means for discovering bluegrass. Continue your journey with these many print, audio, visual, and electronic resources, and you will never be at a loss for expanding your bluegrass horizons.

HISTORY

Books

Bluegrass Breakdown: The Making of the Old Southern Sound
by Robert Cantwell
University of Illinois Press, 1984; 2003 (new preface)

Musical Instruments of the Southern Appalachian Mountains
by John Rice Irwin
Schiffer Publishing, 1983

Bluegrass: A History
by Neil V. Rosenberg
University of Illinois Press, 1985

Bluegrass: An Informal Guide
by Richard D. Smith
Chicago Review Press: a cappella books, 1995

America's Music: Bluegrass. A History of Bluegrass Music in the Words
of Its Pioneers
by Barry R. Willis
1997
Pine Valley Music
73-1400 Hamiha Street
Kailua-Kona HI 96740
http://www.pinevalleymusic.com

Liner Notes

35 Years of the Best in Bluegrass: 1960-1995, Rebel Records 4000
by Bill Vernon

Video

High Lonesome: The Story of Bluegrass Music
by Rachel Liebling
Northside Films, 1991

Bluegrass Museums

International Bluegrass Music Museum
207 East Second Street
Owensboro KY 42303

270-926-7891
888-MY-BANJO
http://www.bluegrass-museum.org

Bill Monroe's Bluegrass Hall of Fame and Country Star Museum
Bill Monroe's Memorial Music Park
5163 State Road 135 North
Bean Blossom IN 46160
800-414-4677
812-988-6422
http://www.beanblossom.com/giftshop/giftshop.html

Ralph Stanley Museum and Traditional Mountain Music Center
Clintwood VA
http://www.ralphstanleymuseum.com
(under construction, scheduled to open in late 2004)

Roots and Branches Museums

Country Music Hall of Fame
222 Fifth Avenue South
Nashville TN 37203
800-852-6437
http://www.countrymusichalloffame.com

Pioneer Music Museum
Main Street
Anita IA 50020
712-762-4363
http://www.oldtimemusic.bigstep.com

Rock and Roll Hall of Fame and Museum
One Key Plaza (East Ninth Street at Lake Erie)
Cleveland OH 44114
216-781-ROCK
http://www.rockhall.com

Out-of-Print Publications and Back Issues

A wealth of historical information can be found in back issues of current publications as well as in the pages of the early seminal bluegrass magazines, *Muleskinner News* and *Pickin'*, both long out of print. Comb your library stacks, watch festival vendor bins, or check out classified ads in *Bluegrass Now* and *Bluegrass Unlimited* as old copies surface from time to time.

KEEPING CURRENT

Print and Online Bluegrass Publications

Bluegrass Guide
164 Church Avenue
Bellow Falls VT 05101
802-463-1184
http://www.bluegrassguide.com

Bluegrass Now
PO Box 2020
Rolla MO 65402
800-736-0125 573-341-7336
http://www.bluegrassnow.com

Bluegrass Unlimited
PO Box 771
Warrenton VA 20188
800-BLU-GRAS
540-349-8181
http://www.bluegrassmusic.com

Bluegrass Works
http://www.bluegrassworks.com

Cybergrass
http://www.cybergrass.com

Discover Bluegrass
http://www.discoverbluegrass.com

GoBluegrass
http://www.gobluegrass.com

ibluegrass
http://www.ibluegrass.com

Women in Bluegrass
PO Box 2498
Winchester VA 22604
800-227-2357 540-877-2357
http://www.murphymethod.com

Nonbluegrass-Exclusive Print and Online Publications

Dirty Linen
PO Box 66600
Baltimore MD 21239
410-583-7973
http://www.dirtylinen.com

Folk Roots
PO Box 337
London N4 1TW, England
44-0-20-8340-9651
http://www.frootsmag.com

Hillbilly-Music.com
http://www.hillbilly-music.com

No Depression
PO Box 31332
Seattle WA 98103
206-706-7342
http://www.nodepression.net

The Old-Time Herald
PO Box 994
Carrboro NC 27510
919-967-7727
http://www.oldtimeherald.org

RootsWorld
http://www.rootsworld.com/rw/

Sing Out!
PO Box 5460
Bethlehem PA 18015
888-SINGOUT
610-865-5366
http://www.singout.org

Festivals

In addition to festival guides and links provided annually or monthly in most publications listed above, the following Internet sites offer additional opportunities to locate bluegrass festivals of every size, shape, and format.

http://www.bluegrassamericana.com

http://www.festivalfinder.com/bluegrass

http://www.festivals.com

http://www.festivals411.com

http://www.musi-cal.com

BROADCASTING

There are literally hundreds of radio programs devoted to bluegrass throughout the United States and Canada, as well as numerous ones abroad. In addition, eclectic shows featuring folk, acoustic, and "alt-country," for example, typically include bluegrass, newgrass, or gospel in their playlists. Public and college-owned stations are often the best sources for this type of programming.

Some shows are now simultaneously streamed on the Internet while on air. Others are re-aired on Internet-based radio sites in lieu of or in addi-tion to syndication on "mortar-and-brick" stations. Internet and satellite radio also offer original programming.

Many print and online publications include radio listings within their pages. Local bluegrass associations can also provide information. Check your area radio station schedules to determine what is available. Use the resources below to dig deeper.

Selected Syndicated Programs

America's Bluegrass, hosted by Bo-Man and Melvin Goins
WTCR 103.3 FM, Catlettsburg KY
http://www.theboman.com/americasbluegrass.html

Banjo Signal, hosted by Trudy Heffernan
KUAC 89.9 FM, Fairbanks AK
http://www.trillmusic.net/banjo.html

Banks of the Ohio, hosted by Fred Bartenstein
WYSO 91.3 FM, Yellow Springs OH
http://www.fredbartenstein.com/radionet.html

The Bluegrass Sound, hosted by Larry Klein
WLTR 91.3 FM, Columbia SC/ETV Radio Network
http:// www.etvradio.org/bgs

Uptown Bluegrass, hosted by George McKnight
Kamloops, BC, Canada
http://www.uptownbluegrass.com

Into the Blue, hosted by Terry Herd
Bluegrass Radio Network, Nashville TN
http://www.bluegrassradio.com

The KingPup Radio Show, hosted by Phil and Gaye Johnson
Aster Productions/Radio YUR, Tryon NC
http://www.radioyur.com/kppg.html

Knee Deep in Bluegrass, hosted by Cindy Baucom
Premiere Radio Network, Charlotte NC
http://www.kneedeepinbluegrass.com

Simply Grass, hosted by Vince Clark
PCCB Productions, Easton PA
http://www.bluegrassmusic.cc

This Is Bluegrass, hosted by Tom Henderson
WMNF 88.5 FM, Tampa Bay FL
http://www.bluegrassparlor.com/links.htm

Internet Radio

http://www.bluegrasscountry.org

http://www.live365.com

http://www.vtuner.com

http://www.virtualtuner.com

Satellite Radio

   Both offer dedicated bluegrass channels.

XM Radio
http://www.xmradio.com

Sirius Satellite Radio
http://www.siriusradio.com

Radio Marketing Service for Program Hosts and Artists

Prime Cuts of Bluegrass
3408 215th Avenue
Keokuk IA 52632
800-638-2286
319-838-2286
http://www.primecutsofbluegrass.com

Acoustic Rainbow Sampler
PO Box 200
Lexington KY 40588
859-225-4020
http://www.acousticrainbow.com

LISTENING TO BLUEGRASS

Live Music

From intimate clubs to large concert venues, one can find live bluegrass, from local to renowned artists. Check the local listings in your newspaper or refer to any of the references cited in "Keeping Current" (previously listed) to locate those close to home.

One exceptional stage is recognized around the globe above all others, and, as such, must be noted. Moreover, because it is located in Music City, U.S.A., you never know who might drop in and sit in with the band. "The World Famous Station Inn" was established in 1974. There is no other place quite like it. Check it out if you have the opportunity.

The Station Inn
402 12th Avenue South
Nashville TN 37203
615-255-3307
http://www.stationinn.com

Record Labels

The following labels represent those that are exclusively bluegrass, primarily bluegrass, or have a large stable of bluegrass artists. Some are very modest in their catalogs, while others are large companies.

In addition, there are many independently produced or self-produced artists who are not affiliated with a record company; one should not dismiss such artists for lack of a "name" label. A handful of well-established artists are among them, as are young bands on the rise.

The following is a list of specialized retail outlets that offer extensive selections of bluegrass music and videos. Of course, most major online and mortar-and-brick music stores carry excellent inventory, too, or can order your choices.

If you are unsure about what to purchase, keep in mind that reissues, compilations, and retrospectives often provide good cross-sections of material and artists. Finally, combing the vinyl and CD bins at festivals is always worth an hour of your time; you are bound to find an out-of-print treasure.

Acoustic Disc
PO Box 4143
San Rafael CA 94913
800-221-DISC
415-454-1187
http://www.acousticdisc.com

Arhoolie Records
10341 San Pablo Avenue
El Cerrito CA 94530
510-525-7471
http://www.arhoolie.com

Bear Family Records
PO Box 1154
27727 Hambergen, Germany
49-4748-82160
http://www.bear-family.de

Bell Buckle Records
PO Box 298
Bell Buckle TN 37020
931-389-9694
http://www.bellbucklerecords.com

B.O.M. Service Ltd.
6-5-18 Kawamo
Takarazuka, Hyogo
665-0842 Japan
81-797-870561
http://www.bomserv.com

CMH Records
PO Box 39439
Los Angeles CA 90039
323-663-8073
http://www.cmhrecords.com

Compass Records
117 30th Avenue South
Nashville TN 37212
615-320-7672
http://www.compassrecords.com

Copper Creek Records
PO Box 3161
Roanoke VA 24015
888-438-2448
540-563-0000
http://www.coppercreekrecords.com

Hay Holler Records
PO Box 868 Blacksburg VA 24063
866-666-7741
540-552-7959
http://www.hayholler.com

Heritage Music Collection
Cracker Barrel Old Country Store
PO Box 787
Lebanon TN 37088
800-333-9566
http://www.crackerbarrel.com/about-heritage.cfm?doc_id=503

June Appal Records
91 Madison
Whitesburg KY 41858
606-633-0108
http://www.appalshop.org

Lonesome Day Records
143 Deaton Road
Booneville KY 41314
606-398-2369
http://www.lonesomedayrecords.com

Native and Fine Records
1185 Solano Avenue PMB #157
Albany CA 94706
510-559-8879
http://www.nativeandfinerecords.com

Old Homestead Records
PO Box 100 Brighton MI 48116
517-548-7772
810-227-1997
http:/ /mywebpages.comcast.net/oldhomestead/

OMS Records
PO Box 52112
Durham NC 27717
888-522-5607
919-846-6120
http://www.omsrecords.com

Pinecastle Records
PO Box 753
Columbus NC 28722
888-473-7773; 828-894-0322
http:/ /www.pinecastle.com

Rebel Records
PO Box 7405
Charlottesville VA 22906
434-973-5151
http:/ /www.rebelrecords.com

Rounder Records
One Camp Street
Cambridge MA 02140
800-ROUNDER
617-354-0700
http:/ /www.rounder.com

Rural Rhythm Records
PO Box 660040
Arcadia CA 91066
800-776-8742
626-286-8742
http:/ /www.ruralrhythm.com

Shanachie Entertainment and Yazoo Records
37 East Clinton Street Newton NJ 07860
800-497-1043
973-579-7763
http:/ /www.shanachie.com

Shell Point Records
330 Franklin Road, Suite 135A-174
Brentwood TN 37027
615-837-6740
http://www.shellpointrecords.com

Sierra Records
PO Box 853
Pasadena CA 91117
800-886-6605 (international fax)
http://www.sierra-records.com

Skaggs Family Records
PO Box 2478
Hendersonville TN 37077
615-264-8877
http://www.skaggsfamilyrecords.com

Smithsonian Folkways Recordings
Center for Folklife and Cultural Heritage
Smithsonian Institution
750 9th Street, NW, Suite 4100
Washington DC 20560
202-275-1144
202-275-1143
http://www.folkways.si.edu

Strictly Country Records
PO Box 628
2130 AP Hoofddorp, The Netherlands
31-297-347-101
http://strictlycountryrecords.com

Sugar Hill Records
PO Box 55300
Durham NC 27717
800-996-4455
919-489-4349
http://www.sugarhillrecords.com

Vanguard Records
2700 Pennsylvania Avenue
Santa Monica CA 90404
800-996-4455
310-829-9355
http://www.vanguardrecords.com

Vestapol Videos
PO Box 802
Sparta NJ 07871
973-729-5544
http://www.guitarvideos.com/vesta/00vesta.htm

Retail Outlets

Americana Internet Music Store
http://www.americanamusicplace.com

County Sales
PO Box 191
Floyd VA 24091
540-745-2001
http://www.countysales.com

Elderly Instruments
1100 North Washington
Lansing MI 48906
888-473-5810
517-372-7890
http://www.elderly.com

Ernest Tubb Record Shop
417 Broadway
Nashville TN 37203
615-255-7503 and
2416 Music Valley Drive
Nashville TN 37214
615-889-2474
http://www.etrecordshop.com

Mid-Continent Music
7713 Kolmar Avenue
Skokie IL 60076
847-674-1867
http://www.midcontinentmusic.com

Music Shed
PO Box 765
Columbus NC 28722
800-473-7773
828-894-2446
http://www.musicshed.com

INSTRUMENT FOCUS AND INSTRUCTION

Instructional Materials

Note that most of the retail outlets listed in the previous section also carry instructional materials.

AcuTab Publications
PO Box 21061
Roanoke VA 24018
540-776-6822
http://www.acutab.com

Hal Leonard Corporation
PO Box 13819
Milwaukee WI 53213
414-774-3630
http://www.halleonard.com

Homespun Tapes
PO Box 340
Woodstock NY 12498
800-338-2737
845-246-2550
http://www.homespuntapes.com

Learn-to-Play.Com
106 Highland Villa Drive
Nashville TN 37211
615-837-6505
http://www.learn-to-play.com

Mel Bay Publications
PO Box 66
Pacific MO 63069
800-863-5229
636-257-3970
http://www.melbay.com

The Murphy Method
PO Box 2498
Winchester VA 22604
800-227-2357
540-877-2357
http://www.murphymethod.com

Musician's Workshop
PO Box 161921
Austin TX 78716
800-543-6125
512-452-8348
http://www.musicians-workshop.com

Stefan Grossman's Guitar Workshop
PO Box 802
Sparta NJ 07871
973-729-5544
http://www.guitarvideos.com

Texas Music and Video
PO Box 16248
Lubbock TX 79490
800-261-3368
806-894-9147
http://www.musicvideo.com

Print and Online Instrument-Focused Publications

Acoustic Guitar
PO Box 767
San Anselmo CA 94979
415-485-6946
http://www.acousticguitar.com

The Autoharp Page
http://www.autoharp.org

Autoharp Quarterly
PO Box 336
New Manchester WV 26056
304-387-0132
http://www.autoharpquarterly.com

Banjo Newsletter
PO Box 3418
Annapolis MD 21403
800-759-7425
410-263-6503
508-645-3648
http://www.banjonews.com

The Bluegrass Guitar Home Page
http://www.bluegrassguitar.com

Co-Mando
http://www.co-mando.com

The Dobro or Resonator Guitar Website
http://www.resoguit.com

Dulcimer Players News
PO Box 2164
Winchester VA 22604
540-678-1305
http://www.dpnews.com

Everything Dulcimer
http://www.everythingdulcimer.com

Fiddler Magazine
PO Box 101
North Sydney, N.S., Canada B2A 3M1
902-794-2558
http://www.fiddle.com

Flatpicking Guitar Magazine
PO Box 2160
Pulaski VA 24301
800-413-8296
540-980-0338
http://www.flatpick.com

Mandolin Magazine
PO Box 13537
Salem OR 97309
503-364-2100
http://www.mandolinmagazine.com

Mandolin Quarterly
Box 2770
Kensington MD 20891
301-530-1749
http://www.mandolincafe.com/strings/

MandoZine
http://www.mandozine.com

The Official World Wide Web Hammered Dulcimer Pages
http://www.rtpnet.org/~hdweb/

Strings
PO Box 767
San Anselmo CA 94979
415-485-6946
http://www.stringsmagazine.com

Selected Academic Programs, Camps, and Extended Workshops

American Banjo Camp
9228 1st Avenue NW
Seattle WA 98117
206-781-5026
http://www.americanbanjocamp.com

Augusta Heritage Center
Davis and Elkins College
100 Campus Drive
Elkins WV 26241
304-637-1350
http://www.augustaheritage.com

Bearfoot Bluegrass Camps for Kids
Box 11-1492
Anchorage AK 99511
907-223-9590
http://www.bearfootbluegrass.com/bcfk.html

Belmont University Bluegrass Ensemble
Department of Visual and Performance Arts
1900 Belmont Boulevard
Nashville TN 37212
615-460-6785
http://www.belmont.edu

Bluegrass at the Beach
PO Box 1616
Port Townsend WA 98368
360-385-6836
http://www.bluegrassatthebeach.com

Bluegrass in the Schools
International Bluegrass Music Association
2 Music Circle South, Suite 100
Nashville TN 37203
888-438-4262
615-256-3222
http://www.ibma.org

Bluegrass, Old-Time, and Country Music Program
Center for Appalachian Studies and Services
East Tennessee State University
Box 70556
Johnson City TN 37614
423-439-5348
http://cass.etsu.edu/bluegrass/

Bluegrass Academy (Adults and Children)
Boston Bluegrass Union
PO Box 650061
West Newton MA 02465
617-782-2251
http://www.bbu.org/ed_home.htm

Colorado Pickin' Camp
PO Box 271
Glenwood Springs CO 81601
970-928-6633
http://www.coloradopickincamp.com

Common Ground on the Hill
McDaniel College
Westminster MD 21157
410-857-2771
http://www.commongroundonthehill.org

fiddlekids
2517 Mira Vista
El Cerrito CA 94530
510-235-0370
http://www.fiddlekids.com

Steve Kaufman Acoustic Kamps
PO Box 1020
Alcoa TN 37701

800-FLATPIK
865-982-3808
http://www.flatpik.com

Mark O'Connor Fiddle Camp
PO Box 110573
Nashville TN 37222
615-941-7426
http://www.markoconnor.com/fiddle.camp/index.html

Nashcamp
PO Box 210396
Nashville TN 37221
888-798-5012
615-952-CAMP
615-952-4040
http://www.nashcamp.com

Rockygrass Academy and Kids Academy
PO Box 769
Lyons CO 80540
800-624-2422
303-823-0848
http://www.planetbluegrass.com

South Plains College
Creative Arts Programs and Camp Bluegrass
1401 College Avenue
Levelland TX 79336
806-894-9611 ext. 2280 or 2492
http://www.southplainscollege.edu/creativearts/

Pete Wernick's Banjo and Jam Camps
7930 Oxford Road
Niwot CO 80503
303-652-8346
http://www.drbanjo.com

Wheeling Park (High School) Bluegrass Band Club
1976 Park View Road
Wheeling WV 26003
304-243-0400
http://wphs.ohio.k12.wv.us

NATIONAL AND INTERNATIONAL ORGANIZATIONS

International Bluegrass Music Association (IBMA)
2 Music Circle South, Suite 100
Nashville TN 37203
888-438-4262; 615-256-3222
http://www.ibma.org

Society for the Preservation of Bluegrass Music of America (SPBGMA)
PO Box 271
Kirksville MO 63501
660-665-7172
http://www.spbgma.com

Roots and Branches Music

Americana Music Association
PO Box 128077
Nashville TN 37212
615-438-7500
http://www.americanamusic.org

Country Music Association
One Music Circle South
Nashville TN 37203
615-244-2840
http://cmaworld.com

Gospel Music Association
1205 Division Street
Nashville TN 37203
615-242-0303
http://www.gospelmusic.org

National Traditional Country Music Association
PO Box 492
Anita IA 50020
712-762-4363
http://www.oldtimemusic.bigstep.com

North American Folk Music and Dance Alliance (The Folk Alliance)
510 South Main
Memphis TN 38103
901-522-1170
http://www.folk.org

CONNECTING WITH BLUEGRASS AROUND THE WORLD

Canada

The Ottawa Valley Bluegrass Music Association, one of approximately forty-five such organizations in Canada, maintains an extensive Canada association contact list on its Internet site.

http://www.valleygrass.ca

Mainland Europe

These two umbrella organizations are gateways to more than twenty countries within Europe that have their own active bluegrass associations.

European Bluegrass Music Association
Steinenweg 8
CH-4133 Pratteln
Switzerland
41-61-8218363
http://www.ebma.org

European World of Bluegrass Association
Busken Huetstraat 25
2394 TD Hazerswoude-Rijndijk
The Netherlands
32-473-663001
http://www.ewob.org

British Isles

British Bluegrass Music Association
61 Coronation Road
Lydiate, Liverpool
L31 2NF United Kingdom
44-151-520-1275
http://www.bbma.net

Scottish Bluegrass Association
2 West Clifton View
East Calder, West Lothian
EH53 0HT Scotland
44-0131-333-5009
http://www.scottishbluegrass.com

Israel

Tzora Folk Club (telephone 972-02-9908382 or 972-051-348061) is one of several regular music series featuring bluegrass, folk, and blues in Israel. Its Internet site is an excellent source for contact and event information, http://www.geocities.com/tzorafolk/index.html

Japan

B.O.M. Service, Ltd., is a long-established, multifaceted bluegrass enterprise that can provide information on several organizations and the many activities within the country.

B.O.M. Service, Ltd.
6-5-18 Kawamo
Takarazuka Hyogo
665-0842 Japan
81-797-870561
http://www.bomserv.com

South America

São Paolo Bluegrass Music Association
Alameda Rouxinol, 601
Aldeia da Serra
Barueri, São Paolo
CEP 06428-010 Brazil
55-11-41-922842
http://www.bluegrass.com.br

Down Under

Bluegrass and Traditional Country Music Society of Australia
http://www.bluegrass.org.au

Wellington Bluegrass Society
36 Beazley Avenue
Paparangi, Wellington
6004 New Zealand
64-4-477-0069

Print and Online Non-U.S. Bluegrass Publications

Bluegrass Europe
(includes *Strictly Country Magazine* and *Bluegrass-Bühne*)
Steinenweg 8
CH-4133 Pratteln
Switzerland
41-61-8218363
http://www.bluegrass-europe.com

Bluegrass North
(inaugural issue slated for Sept./Oct. 2004)
PO Box 44609, Garden Park
Vancouver, BC
V5M 4R8 Canada
604-782-3477
http://www.bluegrassnorthpublishing.com

BlueNa Bluegrass World
http://www.bluegrass.de

Country Store
Casella Postale (PO Box) 1733
20101 Milan, Italy
http://www.bcmai.it/magazine.asp

Moonshiner Bluegrass Journal
6-5-18 Kawamo
Takarazuka Hyogo
665-0842 Japan
81-797-870561
http://www.bomserv.com/moonshiner/index.html

North West Bluegrass News Magazine
http://www.nwbn.freeserve.co.uk

Selected Works Consulted

I am indebted to all my colleagues and predecessors who have studied in depth and written comprehensively about bluegrass, folk, and country, and whose work I have learned from and leaned on. In addition to virtually all of the reference items noted in "Where to from Here" and "Twenty-Five Recordings to Jump Start Your Collection," I have relied on hundreds of Internet sites, scores of liner notes, dozens of back issues of relevant music publications, many personal interviews, and numerous mainstream media clippings. Finally, the following sources were among countless others that were devoured and scoured for background, facts, and interesting tidbits. Many were fascinating; all were insightful. Whenever possible, biographical facts were checked directly with an artist, either relying on his or her personal Internet site or from interviews I have conducted over the years and through the present.[1]

Books: *American Roots Music*, edited by Robert Santelli, Holly George-Warren, Jim Brown (Harry N. Abrams, 2002); *The Bill Monroe Reader*, edited by Tom Ewing (University of Illinois Press, 2000); *Country Music, U.S.A.* by Bill C. Malone (University of Texas Press, 2002); *Country Roots: The Origins of Country Music* by Douglas B. Green (Hawthorn Books, 1976); *Finding Her Voice: The Illustrated History of Women in Country Music* by Mary A. Bufwack and Robert K. Oermann (Henry Holt and Company, 1993); *Folk Festivals: A Handbook for Organization and Management* by Joe Wilson and Lee Udall (University of Tennessee Press, 1982); *Introducing American Folk Music* by Kip Lornell (Brown and Benchmark, 1993); *Southern Music, American Music* by Bill C. Malone (University Press of Kentucky, 1979); *Transforming Tradition: Folk Music Revivals Examined*, edited by

[1]Some books and videos are out of print but may be found in libraries. Others have more recently revised or paperback editions available.

Neil V. Rosenberg (University of Illinois Press, 1993); *Will You Miss Me When I'm Gone? The Carter Family and Their Legacy in American Music* by Mark Zwonitzer with Charles Hirshberg (Simon and Schuster, 2002); *The Women of Country Music: A Reader,* edited by Charles K. Wolfe and James E. Akenson (University Press of Kentucky, 2003).

Videos (DVD and VHS): *America's Music: The Roots of Country,* by Robert K. Oermann and Tom Neff (Turner Home Entertainment, three volumes, 1996; original release 1995); *Appalachian Journey: From the Original Ballad of Tom Dooley to the Origins of Bluegrass,* by Alan Lomax (Vestapol, 1998; original date 1990); *Bluegrass Roots,* by David Hoffman (Varied Directions, 1965); *That High Lonesome Sound: Films of American Rural Life and Music,* by John Cohen (Shanachie Entertainment, 1997; original release 1967).

Index

About the Author

STEPHANIE P. LEDGIN is a journalist and photographer who has focused on bluegrass and traditional folk music since 1975, when she began work as an editor of the seminal bluegrass magazine *Pickin'*. Her work has also appeared in such publications as *Bluegrass Unlimited, Acoustic Guitar, Sing Out!,* and *Bluegrass Now.* Former director of the New Jersey Folk Festival, she is also author-photographer of *From Every Stage: Images of America's Roots Music.*

Music in American Life

Burn, Baby! BURN! The Autobiography of Magnificent Montague
  Magnificent Montague with Bob Baker
Way Up North in Dixie: A Black Family's Claim to the Confederate Anthem
  Howard L. Sacks and Judith Rose Sacks
The Bluegrass Reader   *Edited by Thomas Goldsmith*
Colin McPhee: Composer in Two Worlds   *Carol J. Oja*
Robert Johnson, Mythmaking, and Contemporary American Culture
  Patricia R. Schroeder
Composing a World: Lou Harrison, Musical Wayfarer   *Leta E. Miller and
  Fredric Lieberman*
Fritz Reiner, Maestro and Martinet   *Kenneth Morgan*
That Toddlin' Town: Chicago's White Dance Bands and Orchestras, 1900-1950
  Charles A. Sengstock Jr.
Dewey and Elvis: The Life and Times of a Rock 'n' Roll Deejay   *Louis Cantor*
Come Hither to Go Yonder: Playing Bluegrass with Bill Monroe   *Bob Black*
Chicago Blues: Portraits and Stories   *David Whiteis*
The Incredible Band of John Philip Sousa   *Paul E. Bierley*
"Maximum Clarity" and Other Writings on Music   *Ben Johnston, edited by
  Bob Gilmore*
Staging Tradition: John Lair and Sarah Gertrude Knott   *Michael Ann Williams*
Homegrown Music: Discovering Music   *Stephanie P. Ledgin*

The University of Illinois Press
is a founding member of the
Association of American University Presses.

———————————————————————————

University of Illinois Press
1325 South Oak Street
Champaign, IL 61820-6903
www.press.uillinois.edu